Religious artefacts in the Classroom

A PRACTICAL GUIDE FOR PRIMARY
AND SECONDARY TEACHERS

**by Paul Gateshill
and Jan Thompson**

Hodder & Stoughton

A MEMBER OF THE HODDER HEADLINE GROUP

H144/10

Acknowledgements

The authors would like to thank the following:

Lynne Broadbent for reading and advising on the completed manuscript; Louise and Ian Diamond for checking the accuracy of the Jewish section; Mr Rahman for checking the accuracy of the Islamic section; Mathoor Krishnamurti for checking the Hindu section; Darshan Singh for checking the Sikh section; Mel Thompson for advising on the Buddhist section; Pat Dorbin for the idea behind the article on Memories; the Croydon RE Resource Centre for supplying artefacts to be photographed.

The publishers would like to thank Omnibus Books for permission to publish the extract from *Wilfrid Gordon McDonald Partridge* by Mem Fox.

The publishers would like to thank the following for permission to reproduce copyright photographs in this book: David Rose (front cover; p132); Paul Gateshill (front cover, lower); Colin Izod (p128); Mel Thompson (remainder).

The drawings in the Buddhist section are reproduced by permission of The Friends of the Western Buddhist Order, and were drawn by Dharmachari Aloka.

> In fond memory of
> **KEN OLDFIELD**
> who always encouraged active learning
> and inspired so many of us in
> Religious Education.

British Library Cataloguing in Publication Data
Thompson, Jan
Religious Artefacts in the Classroom
I. Title II. Gateshill, Paul
291.37
ISBN 0 340 57002 4

First published 1992
Impression number   12 11 10 9 8 7 6 5 4
Year   1999 1998 1997 1996 1995

Printed in Great Britain for Hodder & Stoughton Educational, a division of Hodder Headline Plc, 338 Euston Road, London NW1 3BH by The Bath Press, Avon

Contents

Preface

The word 'artefact' may conjure up an image of a dusty relic in a museum, but it literally means any 'product of human art and workmanship' (*The Concise Oxford Dictionary*) and refers to things made for use both in the past and present. A religious artefact is something made for use in religion; and those usually used in RE lessons, and described in this book, are things which are still used by religious people today.

Artefacts of various sorts have always been used by good teachers because pupils naturally enjoy being able to focus on something tangible. Religious Education, perhaps more than any other area of the curriculum, needs to make use of artefacts in the classroom if it wants to motivate pupils who in the main have very little experience of traditional religious practices. So a lesson on the exodus and Passover can be enriched with a Seder plate. Teaching about Easter can make use of examples of the cross appropriate to the age of the pupils, whether it be hot-cross buns or a crucifix. A prayer-mat will help when teaching about Muslim prayer. A display of Hindu images could help pupils appreciate something of the breadth of the Hindu vision of God. A statue of the Buddha could speak to them of the serenity of this religion. When studying the Sikh Five K's, why not show pupils the real things?

This book is for all teachers of RE, whether in Primary or Secondary schools, and is written as much for the non-specialist as for the specialist. It is an attempt to draw together much of the good practice already in existence and to catalogue in one volume information about the main religious artefacts available in Britain today. It explains how they are used within their religions and suggests activities for use in the classroom suitable for different ages. It gives advice on how to obtain such artefacts, and suggests general strategies for using them in RE lessons.

It is our hope that the use of artefacts will enhance the quality of Religious Education in schools by taking its place alongside a variety of other resources and approaches to the subject.

Why and how?

Why use artefacts in Religious Education?

The real thing

Religious artefacts bring pupils into touch with the real thing: the actual objects used by people today in the course of practising their religions. This opportunity to give pupils some first hand experience of religions is particularly important for the many children in our classes who have no direct personal contact with religions .

Interest value

Artefacts tend to arouse interest when brought into a lesson because many are new to the children and fascinating in themselves. Pupils are generally interested to know what these objects are, how they are used and why they are significant.

Easy to remember

When pupils' interest is aroused, they are more likely to remember the learning experience.

Hands-on experience

Children learn by doing; and artefacts give the opportunity for pupils to become actively involved in the lessons e.g. in handling them, making and using them.

Understanding religion in general

Pupils will realise that artefacts have an important place in many religions, both on ritual occasions and in the private devotions of believers.

Artefacts should also help pupils to understand the nature of religious symbolism, since the significance of many an artefact is found not in the object itself but in its underlying meaning. *It is therefore very important that, in using artefacts, we do not fix their attention too firmly on the outward objects, but encourage pupils to think about what they symbolise.* (See p18 where a Christian prosphora seal becomes the focus for an exercise on symbolism.)

Understanding particular religions and the objects they use

The exploration of artefacts from particular religions can help children to understand those religions better.

Affirms faith of believers

Where there are children in the class belonging to a religion whose artefacts are being used, it is hoped that the artefacts will be introduced and used in such a way as to affirm their faith, giving them pride in their own religion.

Better than pictures and photographs

Artefacts can be explored from all angles, whereas pictures show only one face of the object.

Some advantages over videos

Pupils can explore all dimensions of an artefact, as well as seeing and hearing it. They might feel it, lift it up, smell it and taste it. (NB Videos, of course, have different advantages, in that they can show an artefact being used within the faith community. We would not wish to encourage the use of artefacts in the classroom to the exclusion of other media for RE !)

Some advantages over visits to places of worship

Apart from the fact that it is usually easier to show artefacts in school than to arrange a visit, pupils can also take more time over exploring artefacts in school and may feel less inhibited in their exploration.

The end result should be that pupils understand:
- what the religious artefact is;
- how it is used within the faith community;
- the value and importance it has for those who use it i.e. what it tells us about their beliefs.

How to use artefacts in Religious Education

After proper preparation

Teachers must first discover for themselves as much as possible about the artefact and anticipate pupils' questions. They should know how to handle the artefact and if there are any sensitive issues involved e.g. a Qur'an should never be left open on display, since Muslims normally only open it to read it; a kirpan should never be drawn from its sheath in class, since Sikhs only do this when the dagger is to be used.

With respect

We do not want to give offence to those whose religious artefacts we are handling. If the teacher treats religious artefacts with respect and explains that this is because these objects are important to the people who use them, it will encourage pupils to be sensitive to what other people hold sacred. Again, this can be linked with pupil's own experiences. They could be asked to think of something which is very precious to them and of how they would feel is someone ridiculed it or mistreated it.

In the same way as believers (where appropriate!)

Many RE teachers simulate Passover or Baptism, using the objects in the same way as they would be used by believers; but they may not want to involve pupils in making offerings at a Hindu shrine, nor feel comfortable simulating Holy Communion. This needs much thought and sensitivity, with consideration given to the attitude within the religion e.g. Muslims are generally unhappy about pupils going through the prayer motions. But where it is appropriate to use the artefact in the classroom in the same way as it is used by believers, it helps pupils to understand what it means to be a follower of that religion, and to encourage empathy (standing in another person's shoes).

Making links with children's experiences

It is important to link the artefact with the pupil's own experiences so that they do not appear totally strange and irrelevant to them. For example. a font can be compared to a wash-basin; an altar, with everything set out so beautifully and carefully, can be compared to a dinner table which has been laid for a special meal. More fundamentally, we might try to help pupils appreciate the value of artefacts generally in human experience. (See p9 for an idea which links artefacts and memories.)

In displays

Interest can be aroused by a colourful display. Such a display can also communicate the atmosphere of a particular religion, as in a display on Hinduism with bright colours, tinsel, incense, images and a puja tray. A carefully arranged display of religious objects can teach its own lesson, as in an Easter display showing before and after Easter Sunday, the dark and the light aspects of Easter.

Individually

Remember that a great deal can also come from the study of an individual artefact, even something very small such as a Christian lapel badge of a dove or cross.

In a feely-bag

For young children particularly, this will spark their interest and imagination as well as encouraging them to participate by guessing what is in the bag. It will also develop their sense of touch. (This would be a useful approach to RE for pupils in Special Schools.)

Making use of them

This is not the same as making models of something (e.g. a model mosque). Some genuine, simple artefacts can be made by pupils, just as children of the faith communities might make things to use in their religion. For example, Jewish children often make Simchat Torah flags and use them in procession; Hindu children make rangoli patterns. Making artefacts encourages children to think about their meaning, such as what to put on a greeting card for a religious festival.

Encouraging children to question

See how many different questions the children can think of. For example, a string of rosary beads might lead them to ask: Is it a necklace? If not, what is it for? What is it made of? Does it have to be made of this? Does it have to be this colour? Does it have to be this size? Where does it come from? Can you buy them? Does it have a special number of beads? Why are there spaces between the beads? Why are they arranged in sections? Why does it have a cross hanging from it? Who is the mother and child in the picture?

For problem-solving

An artefact can encourage research into the questions: What is it? What religion does it come from? What is it used for? What significance does it have for a believer? (See p21 where an Islamic compass becomes the focus of a problem-solving exercise.)

As a focus for explanations about a religion

An artefact can be used to explain many different things about a religion e.g. a suitable Islamic prayer-mat could be the focus for teaching about Islamic prayer postures, about mosques and Islamic art, about Makkah as a place of pilgrimage, about Muhammad in Madinah etc. (See p28 where the Sikh emblem, the Khanda, becomes the focus for teaching about major Sikh beliefs, Sikh identity, the initiation ceremony, and the gurdwara.)

As a focus for a theme across a number of religions

An artefact could be the starting-point in studying a particular aspect of religions e.g. a statue of the Buddha for founders of religions; a Hindu diva for festivals of light; a Sikh turban for religious costume. (See p16 for an exercise on the Jewish mezuzah as a focus for sacred writings.)

As a focus for religious questions of a more general nature

Sometimes, the purpose is not to start with an example from one religion in order to move to similar examples in other religions, but to raise more general questions. A Christian burial shroud, for example, could lead to general questions about belief about death. (See p26 where the study of a Buddhist prayer-wheel raises all sorts of questions about prayer in general, and not just within this religion.)

As a stimulus to explore feelings

Since religion involves feelings as well as thoughts, the affective side of RE is as important as its intellectual side. Artefacts can help pupils to enter imaginatively into religious experiences. For example, incense, candles and religious music could be used to create a worshipful atmosphere. Or a Christian baptism candle in a box with the words 'To show that you have passed from darkness to light' could stimulate thought on examples of this common human experience of passing from despair to hope, from sadness to joy.

Linked with other subjects

(See p26 where the exercise with the Buddhist prayer-wheel shows how RE can be linked with Technology; and p24 where the exercise with a statue of Shiva shows how RE can be linked with the arts.)

To raise evaluative questions

Some artefacts raise questions of a general nature for pupils to consider and give their views. For example, the five K's of Sikhism have a military origin and this could lead to discussion on the ethics of using violence, even in defence.

For revision

The teacher could ask questions about the artefact or questions based on it, to demonstrate pupils' recall. Or pupils could be asked to show their understanding by choosing the correct artefacts to illustrate a point. For example, they could be asked to pick out from a box on Judaism all the artefacts to do with worship, and to explain how they contribute to Jewish worship.

A way in to religious artefacts: Memories

Everyday artefacts can be used which may have an implicit or explicit link with Religious Education.

An example of this is well illustrated in the book *Gordon Wilfrid Macdonald Partridge* by Mem Fox. Although this is a children's story, it could be used with practically any age group: from 5 to 99 year olds! It is about memories.

Gordon is a young Australian boy who makes friends with the residents of an old people's home next door. He is particularly fond of Miss Nancy Alison Delacourt Cooper because she too has four names. One day he overhears his parents saying that Miss Nancy has lost her memory. He begins to explore what memories mean and receives the following responses from some of the old people.
A memory is:

> **"Something warm, my child, something warm."**
>
> **"Something from long ago, me lad, something from long ago."**
>
> **"Something that makes you cry, me boy."**
>
> **"Something that makes you laugh, my darling."**
>
> **"Something as precious as gold, young man."**

In order to help Miss Nancy find her memory he seeks out four artefacts which hold memories for him and gives each one to the old lady. Each artefact does in fact trigger memories and Miss Nancy rediscovers her past. It is a delightful and profound story which is beautifully illustrated.

Activities

Some of the following exercises could be used to develop the idea of memories - depending upon the age group of the pupils.

• After hearing the story ask the pupils to reflect on some of the definitions of memories given by the old people.

• In order to explain these definitions, what experiences could each old person have gone through? e.g. What might have happened to the person who said "Something that makes you cry.."?

• Choose a character and relate one such event or story in reasonable detail either in the first or third person.

• You may wish to play some music while the pupils reflect, such as 'Memories' from the musical *CATS*.

• Pupils may then share their responses with each other and then as a whole class.

• Ask your pupils to bring in (or choose from a selection on a table) their own artefact which holds a particular memory for them. They can share with a friend why they have chosen this particular object and its significance. This could be done in writing or art first and then shared.

From implicit to explicit

The above areas are implicit RE, but there are many possibilities for developing this area into more explicit RE. For example a Jewish Seder dish could be introduced to the class as an artefact which is about memories (of the Exodus event). The salt water, for example, reminds Jews of the tears their ancestors shed in Egypt, and of the miraculous crossing of the Sea of Reeds. In fact all festivals are concerned with the community remembering events of the past within the present.

Moving from the implicit to the explicit in this way, from everyday artefacts to religious artefacts, pupils are able to explore the feelings of religious believers and not just the facts about the religion concerned. In the example given, Passover does not remain an academic exercise about what each food represents, but introduces a dimension to help develop empathy within the pupils.

Beg, borrow and ...

Beg

You will be surprised how willing people are to help provide religious artefacts if only you have the cheek to ask! Contact local places of worship with a letter on school paper and ask to meet the person in charge. Do not use the words 'religious artefacts', which can be confusing, but explain the sort of things you need in order to make the teaching of their religion that much more interesting and realistic. Many religious centres, like mosques and gurdwaras, are very generous with booklets about their religions, but they may not think in terms of religious artefacts. You will need to suggest to them the sort of things which would be useful, asking particularly for things which are of no more use to them, either because they are outdated or spare, but which could enrich your pupils' understanding of religions.

From a synagogue

A friendly rabbi may well help by appealing to the congregation for examples of the following:

* Spare Bar/Bat Mitzvah invitation cards
* Spare Wedding invitation cards
* Used Rosh Hashanah cards
* The 'four species' of plants after their use at Sukkot

From a church

* Outdated copies of the church magazine

There is a mine of information in these from which children can learn about the life of the parish. In particular, there will be a list of all the people who help run the church and a list of services.

* Prayer sheets
* Bible tracts

* Letters from missionaries
* Outdated cards/ leaflets advertising Easter or Christmas services
* Baptism certificate
* Spare charity collection box
* Left over palm crosses
* An empty wine bottle labelled for use at Holy Communion
* Holy Communion wafers

These can usually only be bought in bulk, but a friendly clergyman should be willing to let you have a few small communicant's wafers and a large priest's wafer. They will not be consecrated and you will therefore have no worries about offending believers by using them for RE.

* Votive candles
* Some grains of incense

Again, incense can usually only be bought in bulk, so you will have to ask at the church if they can spare you a little (although shops may have some sample packs that they are prepared to let you have).

From a mosque

* A prayer timetable
* Eid cards
* Booklets about aspects of Islam
* Travel-agent posters about Hajj

From a Hindu temple

* Spare wedding invitation cards
* Posters about celebrations such as Divali
* Divali cards

- Wall calendars with pictures of Hindu Deities

From a Buddhist temple

- Booklets on Buddhist philosophy

- Postcards of Buddhas

From a Sikh gurdwara

- Spare wedding invitation cards

- Posters connected with festivals such as Baisakhi

- Literature with examples of Punjabi writing

Borrow

If you have an RE centre within easy reach then you should have access to a wide range of resources. Find out what is available. Sometimes arrangements can be made to post things to schools, especially via an internal mailing system.

It might also be possible to borrow things from local places of worship. For example, a church might lend you some vestments, a hassock, or palm branches which they keep for Palm Sunday. A synagogue might lend you a wedding chuppah.

Buy

Obviously, religious artefacts can be bought from the shops where the faith communities buy them.

Christian clergy and ministers go to church suppliers such as Mowbrays or Wippells for things ranging from a bishop's mitre to altar candles. Some Christian bookshops stock things suitable for a variety of denominations. Many Catholic Churches have stalls for worshippers to buy such things as rosary beads, crucifixes, medallions and little water stoups. These can also be purchased at pilgrimage centres. Don't forget that cards for religious festivals like Christmas

and Easter, and for rites of passage such as Christenings and weddings, can be bought in ordinary shops.

The Salvation Army has its own suppliers. Send for the Souvenirs Catalogue from:

Salvationist Publishing and Supplies Ltd.
117-121 Judd Street
King's Cross
London WC1H 9NN

There are shops in Jewish areas which supply Jewish families with all they need to fulfil their religious requirements, from cards to articles of clothing. There is also a small shop in Woburn House, London, where the Board of Deputies of British Jews and the Jewish Museum can also be found. This shop is used by both Jews and Gentiles, and a 10% discount is given on school orders:

Jewish Memorial Council Bookshop,
Woburn House,
Upper Woburn Place,
London WC1H OEP.

Another source for Jewish artefacts, which is mail order (visits by appointment) is:

Jewish Education Bureau
8 Westcombe Avenue
Leeds LS8 2BS

It may also be possible to buy Jewish greetings cards, especially Rosh Hashanah cards, in non-religious card shops.

Most big mosques have stalls for Muslims to buy copies of the holy Qur'an, prayer mats and so on. There is also a wide range of Muslim articles available by visit or by post, with a discount for schools, from:

Muslim Information Services
233 Seven Sisters Road
London N4 2DA.

Buddhist centres usually have postcards and Buddha images for sale.

This mail order company has a wide range of statues, incense, posters, cards. and stickers:

Tantra Designs
Gas Ferry Road
Bristol BS1 6UN

You will find drapery shops in Hindu and Sikh areas where you can buy sarees, shalwar kameez and dupattas, and material for turbans. Hardware shops will sell puja trays, divas, images and Sikh symbols. A local newsagent may have brightly coloured Hindu posters of their many deities and children's comics telling the famous stories about them. Markets in these areas are also well worth visiting.

As far as we know, the only business set up as an educational supplier (by mail order) of artefacts for RE on many different religions is:

Articles of Faith
Christine and Leslie Howard
Bury Business Centre
Kay Street
Bury
Lancashire BL9 6BU
Tel. 061 705 1878

For Hindu, Sikh and Muslim artefacts, you could visit or order by post from:

'Little India'
91 the Broadway
Southall
Middlesex UB1 1LN
Tel. 081 571 2029

There are, however, a number of Multi-Cultural Centres and Language Units which sell a variety of useful things for RE, which can usually be bought on mail-order.

Finally, don't ignore the humble charity shops where all sorts of interesting items can turn up and where you might find appropriate drapes to display your religious artefacts. They may also stock useful artefacts made in Third World countries, such as incence and joss-stick holders.

Make

It is possible to make many RE artefacts, though this will depend on your time, inclination and skill, the willingness of others to help you and the friendliness of the textile, woodwork and metalwork departments in your school.

Some examples are suggested in the Activities sections in Part 2 of this book.

Using religious artefacts in the classroom

The sections that follow look at various ways in which artefacts can be used to enhance Religious Education.

An example is given for each of the following world religions:

Christianity - using artefacts to explore the use of symbol in religion

Judaism - using artefacts to explore sacred writings

Islam - using artefacts as a problem solving activity

Hinduism - using artefacts to explore the links between religion and art

Buddhism - using artefacts to explore the links between religion and technology

Sikhism - using an artefact as an opening to the study of a particular religion.

Before an examination of each of these in detail, here is an example of one lesson where religious artefacts were used to their full potential. This example was with year 6 primary pupils who were studying a topic entitled "Lifestyle".

1.   Introduction:

Class discussion around the question "What do we already know about how religion affects the ways in which people live their lives?" These ideas were written on a central chart for future reference.

2.   Activity:

Children worked in small groups (4-6) with artefacts linked with lifestyle
e.g. Group 1 had artefacts associated with Islamic prayer (see page 89f).
Group 2 had artefacts associated with Jewish Shabbat (see page 38f).
Group 3 had the 5 K's of Sikhism (see page 132f).
Group 4 had a Hindu Puja tray (see page 108).
Group 5 had artefacts associated with Christian baptism (see page 67f).
Before pupils handled the objects they were given the following instructions:
• remember that these objects are special to the people that they belong to, so treat them with respect.

• you have ten minutes to look at the objects and to work out:

> what religion they might belong to,
>
> what they might be used for and
>
> what they might tell us about religion and lifestyle.

In this activity the teacher made sure that children were not at a table which contained artefacts of their own religion. This was simply to enhance the problem-solving nature of this session.

3. Presentation:

Each group in turn made a presentation of their findings to the whole class. Some ideas were the fruit of good detective work and others were ingenious in their imagination. For example the group looking at Islamic prayer were on the right track but thought that the compass might be an instrument for counting how many times Muslims had prayed during the day. The teacher commended them for their thinking but suggested that they do some more research on the matter. It would have been easy for the teacher to give them all the answers on a plate at this point, but that would have taken away the mystery surrounding the object and thereby diminished the pupils' innate curiosity.

4. Research:

Pupils continued to work in their groups, but this time they were given extra resources in order to deepen their investigation. These resources included text books, posters and pamphlets. They were told that they had one hour in which to find out more about the objects and to prepare a final presentation of their findings. This presentation was to include drawings of the artefacts and written information, and/or a prepared script for an oral presentation. The teacher moved from group to group suggesting ways in which they might find out more information. Sometimes the skilful use of questioning helped pupils to deepen their research.

5. Final presentations:

After lunch the class was refreshed and eager to share their work with the other groups. The teacher had decided to break up each presentation with short video extracts (lasting 2-3 minutes) on the areas being studied by the children. This served to reinforce the children's own presentations and to lead to further discussion with the whole class. At the end of the session, the children were beginning to think quite deeply in a discussion which explored why it was important to know about other people's customs, beliefs and religious practices.

Although this activity lasted a whole day it could be rearranged so as to be suitable for Secondary school timetables. Some Primary staff may question the validity of spending so much time on RE. There is, however, a wealth of cross curricular work covered within this activity: language development, artwork, geography, maths and of course developing skills of research, oracy, collaboration and so on.

Teachers involved in this activity have commented on:

• the motivation of the pupils. The artefacts added a new dimension to the learning experience. The mystery surrounding the various objects increased the motivation of pupils and this was evident in the quality of the work produced for the presentation.

• pupils' prior knowledge. Teachers are often amazed at how much their pupils already know. Perhaps the tangible nature of the artefacts themselves sparks off all sorts of ideas and experiences which the pupils are able to piece together collectively.

• the videos. Clips from the videos enable the pupils to see how the artefacts are used by the adherents of a particular faith. This reinforces their learning.

Artefacts and sacred writings: Jewish mezuzah

There are many artefacts which are associated with the different Sacred Writings. For example: the Sikh chauri which is a fan waved over the Guru Granth Sahib, the wooden Qur'an stand used by Muslims, the yad or pointer used by Jews when reading from the Torah, and so on. In this section we will concentrate on the mezuzah, a Jewish artefact which contains a portion of the Jewish scriptures.

If you visit a Jewish household you may notice a small box attached to the right hand front door post. It is about 10 by 4 cms in size and attached at eye level. This is a mezuzah case.

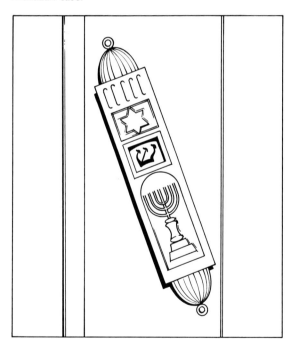

The mezuzah contains a piece of parchment which has verses from the Jewish Bible (Tenach) handwritten in Hebrew. On the front are sections from Deuteronomy 6 v4-9 and 11 v13-21 and on the back the word "Shaddai" (Almighty). Sometimes the mezuzah will have a hole in it so that the word "Shaddai" can be seen. If it does not, then the word "Shaddai" or the letter "shin" will be written on the front of the container.

The mezuzah originates from the famous Jewish prayer known as the Shema. (Deuteronomy 6 v4-9)

"Shema Yisrael, Adonai Eloheynu, Adonai Echad..."

"Hear O Israel: The Lord our God The Lord is one; and you shall love the Lord your God with all your heart, and with all your soul, and with all your might. And these words which I command you this day shall be upon your heart ... and you shall write them on the doorposts of your house and on your gates."

The word mezuzah actually means "door post" and Orthodox Jewish homes will not only have a mezuzah on the front door post but also at the entrance of every room in the house apart from the bathroom and toilet. Jews touch the mezuzah on passing through the doorway and kiss their fingers. This suggests the importance of the home and the family in Judaism. The home is where many of the major festivals take place and where Shabbat is observed weekly. The mezuzah reminds Jews to put God first in their homes.

Here is a reproduction of the parchment which is rolled up inside the mezuzah.

שמע ישראל יהוה אלהינו יהוה אחד ואהבת אית
יהוה אלהיך בכל לבבך ובכל נפשך ובכל מאדך והיו
הדברים האלה אשר אנכי מצוך היום על לבבך ושננתם
לבניך ודברת בם בשבתך בביתך ובלכתך בדרך
ובשכבך ובקומך וקשרתם לאות על ידך והיו לטטפת
בין עיניך וכתבתם על מזזות ביתך ובשעריך
                        והיה אם שמע תשמעו אל מצותי אשר אנכי
מצוה אתכם היום לאהבה את יהוה אלהיכם ולעבדו
בכל לבבכם ובכל נפשכם ונתתי מטר ארצכם בעתו
יורה ומלקוש ואספת דגנך ותירשך ויצהרך ונתתי
עשב בשדך לבהמתך ואכלת ושבעת השמרו לכם
פן יפתה לבבכם וסרתם ועבדתם אלהים אחרים
והשתחויתם להם וחרה אף יהוה בכם ועצר את
השמים ולא יהיה מטר והאדמה לא תתן את יבולה
ואבדתם מהרה מעל הארץ הטבה אשר יהוה נתן לכ
ושמתם את דברי אלה על לבבכם ועל נפשכם וקשרתם
אתם לאות על ידכם והיו לטוטפת בין עיניכם ולמדתם
אתם את בניכם לדבר בם בשבתך בביתך ובלכתך
בדרך ובשכבך ובקומך וכתבתם על מזוזות ביתך
ובשעריך למען ירבו ימיכם וימי בניכם על האדמה
אשר נשבע יהוה לאבתיכם לתת להם כימי השמים
על הארץ

Activities and areas to explore

• Pupils may wish to make their own mezuzah. They can copy out Deuteronomy 6 v4-5 and then design a container which can be decorated with Jewish symbols.

• Older pupils may be able to explore the central ideas contained within the Shema. It enshrines the heart of Jewish belief such as the complete one-ness of God.

• The Shema is also contained in the tefillin or phylacteries worn by Orthodox Jewish males during weekday morning prayer.

> "And you shall bind them as a sign upon your hand, and they shall be as frontlets between your eyes." (Deuteronomy 6 v8)

It may be possible to invite a Jewish visitor to the classroom to talk about the mezuzah and perhaps even to demonstrate how the tefillin are worn. An interview could be set up which explores questions such as:

"What does it mean to you when you touch the mezuzah?"

"How do you feel when you put on the tefillin?"

• The class may be able to build up a collection of artefacts which are linked with the Sacred Writings of different religions.

For example:

Judaism: mezuzah, tefillin (phylacteries), megillah, yad, miniature Torah

Islam: Qur'anic wooden stand and cloth cover

Christianity: Bible study notes with suggested daily readings

Sikhism: chauri and romalla set

Hinduism: commentary on the Bhagavad Gita

Buddhism: Prayer wheel.

Associated with the setting up of this exhibition should be the constant question:

"What do these artefacts tell us about the attitude of believers to their own Sacred Writings?"

This may need to be drawn out by asking more direct questions such as: "Why do Jews use a metal pointer? Why don't they just use their finger?" and so on.

Religious Artefacts and Symbols: Christian Prosphora Seal.

The Prosphora seal is an inexpensive and intriguing artefact. It can be introduced as a mystery object and pupils can work out for themselves what it is used for. Usually someone in the group will suggest that it is used to make some form of imprint. Some may even suggest that it is a butter pat or seal. They will however, experience more difficulty trying to work out what religion it belongs to!

The Prosphora seal is in fact a Christian artefact from the Greek Orthodox tradition. It is a wooden implement for making an imprint on the "Prosphora" which is the bread used for the Divine Liturgy (in other traditions called the Mass, Eucharist, Holy Communion).

It is considered a great honour for a family to make the Prosphora bread to give to the priest before the service and can only be performed by a devout and upright family. The actual making of the bread itself is full of ritual and is accompanied by prayers.

The Prosphora seal is evidence of the tremendously rich use of symbol and ritual within the Orthodox Church.

The seal itself can be divided into five squares arranged in the form of a cross. However, because the seal is a mirror image, the symbols can only be identified by actually making an imprint. This could be with paint on paper or on dough as originally intended.

N.B. It is essential to seal the wood first with linseed oil or the wood will swell and the symbols will disappear!

When you have your imprint you should be able to identify the following:

I C	X C
N I	K A

Sometimes these are abbreviated as I, X, N, K.

This is Greek and stands for

I C	Jesus
X C	Christ
N I K A	Conqueror

This square is known as "the Lamb" and is the only part of the bread which is Consecrated and "becomes the Body and Blood of Christ through the action of the Holy Spirit." The I C, N I, and K A sections are used for the communion of the people and the X C section is reserved for the priest.

At the beginning of the service the prosphora bread is cut up by the priest. He removes "the Lamb" and places it on a plate called a "paten". He then cuts a triangle section out of the square on the left, thinking of the Virgin Mary as he does so. Next he cuts out the nine triangles on the right and remembers the nine orders of saints. He will place these on the right of the Lamb on the paten. He will then remember the living and the dead by name and will take a crumb for each person and place it on the paten. The paten is then veiled ready for the service of the Divine Liturgy.

Activities

• Pupils may wish to explore some of these ancient symbols and, more importantly, to examine their significance for the majority of Christians. There are those which come from the Greek language, and others such as the cross, the anchor, the dove, the lily and many more. This could be achieved through a visit to an Orthodox, Roman Catholic or Anglican church. Symbols can be found on the priest's vestments, on stained glass windows, on hassocks or kneelers, on statues, on tombstones and of course in the actual shape of some churches.

• Pupils may also be encouraged to examine why some Christian denominations do not make so much use of symbol and imagery in their worship.

• Pupils may explore the use of food in religions, such as the giving out of Prashad at the end of Sikh worship (see page 137), or the symbolic foods used in the Jewish Seder meal (see page 41f). Hopefully pupils will have opportunities to cook and taste some of these foods themselves.

Many Christian symbols originate from Greek words, because Greek was the common language of the ancient world at the time of Jesus.(e.g.the New Testament was originally written in Greek.) Here are the letters of the Greek alphabet most commonly used in Christianity:

A Ω   Alpha and Omega

These are the first and last letters of the Greek alphabet, and are used as a title for Christ to express the Christian belief that he existed before time began and will continue to live for all eternity. It is based on the passage:

"I am the Alpha and the Omega, the first and the last, the beginning and the end." (Revelations 22:13)

$$X + P = \text{Khi-rho}$$ Khi-rho

Khi-ro is an anagram of the first two letters (chi and rho) of Christ in Greek. It has become a common symbol for Christianity.

$$I \, X \, \Theta \, Y \, \Sigma$$ Ichthus

Ichthus is the Greek word for fish. It became a secret symbol used by Christians on the walls of catacombs during Roman persecution, as its letters make up a simple statement of Christian belief:

I	=	Iesus for Jesus
ch	=	Christos for Christ
th	=	Theou for God's
u	=	Uios for Son
s	=	Soter for Saviour

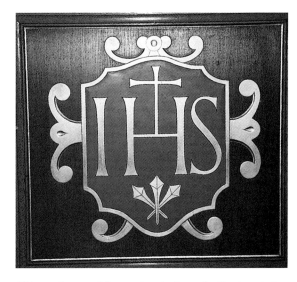

This wooden panel from a church shows the Greek capital letters IHS, which are the first three letters of the name Jesus, and the symbol of the cross above the 'H' (pronounced as an 'e').

Artefacts and problem-solving exercises: The Islamic Compass

Religious artefacts are ideal for problem-solving activities in the classroom. This is because many of them are unfamiliar objects outside of pupils' everyday experience. The artefact often arouses their innate curiosity and therefore presents the teacher with an enthusiastic learner! A problem-solving exercise can be a useful way of beginning a whole unit of work as the following exercise illustrates:

This is an exercise for pupils aged eight and above. Obviously different learning outcomes will emerge depending upon the age and experience of the pupils concerned.

The compass illustrated here comes as a complete package for about £5.00 and includes a compass, box and instructions.

Suggested Activity

Give a small group of pupils the compass (without the instructions) and ask them what they can find out about:

• the religion associated with the artefact

• the name of the artefact

• how it is used and what it is used for

• what it tells us about some of the beliefs and practices of this particular religion

Issues arising:

When this exercise has been used in the classroom, teachers are often amazed at how much children already know and how they are able to piece together small bits of information in order to build up a considerable picture about a particular object. Sometimes however, pupils will get stuck and teachers can feed in one or two clues to keep the activity flowing (e.g. pointing pupils towards useful resources for reference).

When pupils have reached some form of agreement on how to use the compass to find the direction of Makkah, then they can have access to the instructions. These will either confirm the findings of the group or set them right!

The instructions enable Muslims to set the compass from whichever part of the world they are in and then know the precise direction of the Kaaba (Qibla) at Makkah. On the next page you will find a typical set of instructions:

QIBLA DIRECTION FINDER-WORLD WIDE
The Scientific Boussole

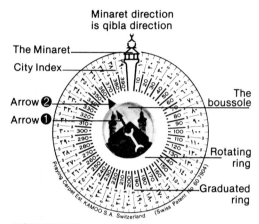

Minaret direction
is qibla direction

The Minaret

City Index

Arrow ❷

Arrow ❶

The boussole

Rotating ring

Graduated ring

HOW TO USE

① Place the Qibla Direction Finder in your hand 1 meter above the floor level and far from metallic object.

② From the guide book select the city and its index number.

③ Move with your finger the rotating ring so its arrow ❷ coincides with the index number of the city.

④ Turn around so that the arrow ❶ of the boussole coincides with the arrow ❷ and the city index number.

⑤ Now the Minaret points to the direction of Qibla.

© Swiss Patent

UNITED KINGDOM		المملكة المتحدة	
250	Belfast	بيلفاست	٢٥٠
250	Cambridge	كيمبرج	٢٥٠
245	Edinburgh	أدنبره	٢٤٥
240	Aberdeen	أبردين	٢٤٠
250	Oxford	أوكسفورد	٢٥٠
255	Liverpool	ليفربول	٢٥٥
255	Sheffield	شيفيلد	٢٥٥
250	Bristol	بريستول	٢٥٠
250	Cardiff	كارديف	٢٥٠
250	Leeds	ليدز	٢٥٠
250	Newcastle	نيوكاسل	٢٥٠
250	Southampton	سوث هامبتون	٢٥٠
250	Birmingham	برمنجهام	٢٥٠
245	Glasgow	جلاسجو	٢٤٥
255	Manchester	مانشستر	٢٥٥
250	Bradford	برادفورد	٢٥٠
250	London	لندن	٢٥٠

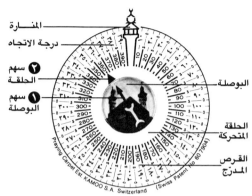

المنـارة

درجة الاتجاه

❷ سهم الحلقة

❶ سهم البوصلة

البوصلة

الحلقة المتحركة

القرص المـدرج

كيفيـة الاستعمـال

① ضع البوصلة على راحة اليد مترا فوق الأرض وبعيدة عن اية قطع معدنية.

② اختار المدينة ودرجة الاتجاه في كتيب ـ دليل درجات الاتجاه للقبلة.

③ دور الحلقة المتحركة بحيث يطابق سهمها رقم ❷ مع درجة الاتجاه للمدينة المختارة.

④ تحرك بحيث يطابق سهم البوصلة رقم ❶ مع سهم الحلقة رقم ❷ ودرجة الاتجاه المطلوبة للمدينة.

⑤ الآن اتجاه المنارة هو اتجاه القبلة.

Some questions to supplement the exercise may be:

1) What number would you set the dial to if you were a Muslim in Nicosia (Cyprus)? London (United Kingdom)?...

2) How many times do Muslims pray during the day?

   What does this tell us about Islam and the Muslim attitude to prayer?

3) Why do Muslims face Makkah when they pray? There are of course various answers to this question...

This exercise could lead on to a whole study about Islam or an aspect of Islam such as prayer. There are many cross curricular links here as well:

Mathematics: We get our number system from the Arab world (especially the use of the zero). Pupils may well be able to match the Arabic and English numbers from the information given in the Qibla Direction instructions.

Pupils familiar with algebra will be interested to discover that this comes from the Arabs too.

Geometric design emerged from the Islamic prohibition of idolatry and all images.

Science: Islam's desire to know as much as possible about the world that Allah created led Muslims to make immense contributions to science in the field of navigation, astronomy, measuring time and so on.

Conclusion

Using a simple and inexpensive artefact such as the compass in the above problem-solving exercise can lead to a whole wealth of learning through pupils' own investigations: e.g.

Islam is a world wide religion

The unity and brotherhood of all believers is an important aspect of Islam

Prayer is one of the 5 pillars of Islam

Islam has made valuable contributions to our own culture

The method of learning in this exercise is also valuable. It involves:

Group co-operation through discussion

Decision making

Research

Handling artefacts with respect

Religious artefacts and the creative arts: Shiva Nataraja - the Lord of the Dance

This is a statue of Shiva, one of the main deities in Hinduism. Here Shiva is seen performing his cosmic dance in which he simultaneously creates and destroys so that he can re-create once again. This aspect of Shiva is known as Shiva Nataraja (Lord of the Dance). Shiva, although he is the god of destruction, is loved as well as feared. This is because Hindus believe in reincarnation, the endless wheel of death and rebirth. The goal of Hinduism is 'moksha' that is release from rebirth and union with the Absolute or Brahman. Death is to be welcomed as being a chance to reach a yet higher state of perfection, and one step closer to 'moksha'.

The statue of Shiva Nataraj is full of symbolism.

• In his cosmic dance he has four arms:

In his upper right arm Shiva holds a drum whose beat represents the sound which brought about creation.

In his upper left arm he holds the flame which symbolises the destruction of the universe.

The gestures of the hands from the lower arms represent that life and death are held rhythmically in a state of balance.

• His right foot treads on the demon/dwarf of ignorance and forgetfulness, while his left foot is raised in dance. This is supposed to represent the stream of consciousness from knowledge to ignorance to knowledge; from birth to death to rebirth.

• The arc of flames represents the whole universe which depends upon Shiva's cosmic dance. All life must be destroyed in order for it to be recreated. There has to be an on-going process of life, death and rebirth.

Activities

The drum that Shiva holds represents the sound which brought about creation. This idea is found in the ancient Hindu writings of the Vedas. It can also be found in more contemporary writings such as *The Magician's Nephew* by C S Lewis. The following passage describes the creation of Narnia by Aslan the Lion:

> The Lion was pacing to and fro about that empty land and singing his new song. It was softer and more lilting than the song by which he had called up the stars and the sun; a gentle, rippling music. And as he walked and sang the valley grew green with grass. It spread out from the Lion like a pool... Polly was finding the song more and more interesting because she thought she was beginning to see the connection between the music and the things that were happening. When a line of dark firs sprang up on a ridge about a hundred yards away she felt they were connected with a series of deep, prolonged notes which the Lion had sung a second before.

And also in *The Silmarillion* by J R R Tolkein

> In the beginning Eru, the One, who in the Elvish tongue is named Iluvatar, made the Ainur of his thought; and they made a great Music before him. In this music the World was begun.

Pupils may wish to explore this idea of the creative power of music. They may even be able to write and perform their own 'creation music'. Perhaps other pupils may wish to explore the idea of creation through movement and dance. Art too can be used to explore Shiva Nataraja. Apart from drawing the statue and exploring the symbols associated with him, pupils could express their ideas about creation and death through art and craft. This may provide opportunities for pupils to explore their own inner feelings about these issues. This obviously demands great sensitivity on behalf of the teacher. It may even be possible to combine all these ideas to present a class production to the rest of the school in an assembly or other suitable function.

Religious artefacts and technology: Buddhist prayer-wheel

A Tibetan Buddhist prayer-wheel

In Tibetan and Bhutanese Buddhism, prayer is constant. It is so integral to life that machines have been invented to make perpetual prayer. Winds, rivers and other forms of energy are harnessed to turn the wheels of prayer. Prayers do not just have to be said by human beings, nature too can pray. If you go to Tibet or Bhutan you will see prayer flags fluttering constantly in the wind. Rivers turn huge prayer wheels which, instead of grinding corn or generating electricity, generate prayers. The wheels contain tens of thousands of prayers which are evoked with just one turn. There is something ecological about the philosophy behind this: Nature and Humanity are at one in the spiritual quest.

The picture here shows a Tibetan prayer-wheel. It contains parchments with various prayers written upon it. The prayers are said by simply turning the wheel. This is acheived by using a technique similar to waving a football rattle. The prayers are various but often a single phrase is repeated over and over again. The idea is that merit is amassed through constant prayer: the more one prays, the more merit is achieved. This is why technology has been exploited to create vast prayer machines which almost pray by themselves. A million prayers can be said in a matter of minutes - technology serving religion.

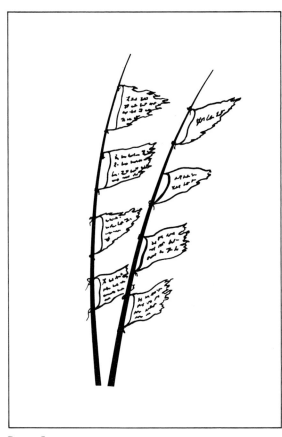

Prayer flags

Activities

• A Tibetan Prater wheel costs about £25.00 in the UK. It is not one of the easiest artefacts to find, but if there is difficulty in finding one for the classroom, there are posters and videos of prayer wheels and other Buddhist prayer machines.

• Perhaps a good secular comparison to the Tibetan prayer-wheel would be the Dream Jars in Roald Dahl's *The BFG*. This may well provide a useful entry point into this whole area of study.

• After talking about the concept of the prayer-wheel, ask pupils to design their own prayer machines using readily available junk material such as toilet roll holders, squeezy bottles etc.. They should be simply powered by using energy such as that supplied by an elastic band, candle and so on.

• Pupils should be given the opportunity to reflect and to make their own choice whether or not they would include a prayer, or a wish, or a dream to be set in motion by the machine. This respects their own integrity by allowing them to respond at their own level.

• Apart from the obvious links with technology, the most important learning experience for the RE teacher is the conversation that naturally emerges about the whole concept of prayer. While pupils are making their own machines they should be encouraged to ask questions such as:

What is prayer ?

Who is prayer for ?

Does prayer work ?

Is prayer a good thing ?

Is there a difference between a prayer and a wish ?

Is turning a wheel of prayer as valuable as actually saying a prayer ?

Are there different types of prayer ?

Using an artefact to introduce a religion: Sikh Khanda

In this section we explore how a religious artefact may provide an unusual and stimulating way-in to the study of a particular religion.

For example, we could base most of our studies of Sikhism on the Khanda, the Sikh emblem which is found on their badges and flags.

The symbol illustrated here is in itself made up of three symbols:

(i) the double edged sword (Khanda)

(ii) the circle (Chakkar)

(iii) the two swords (Kirpan)

(i) The double edged sword or Khanda at the centre is used during the Amrit ceremony which is the Sikh initiation rite (see page. 136f). This symbol could therefore offer opportunities for pupils to look at Sikh rites of passage, especially initiation. It could also lead pupils to investigate the forming of the Khalsa brotherhood by Guru Gobind Singh.

(ii) The circle or Chakkar represents infinity because a circle has no beginning and no end. It points the Sikh to the One God who is Timeless and Absolute. The circle is also a symbol of restraint and reminds Sikhs to remain within the Will of God. Again this symbol could enable pupils to explore what Sikhs believe about God and also how they should live out their lives, in other words an investigation into Sikh ethics.

(iii) The two swords or Kirpans on either side represent the two types of power and authority. One represents Peeri (spiritual power) and the other Meeri (political or earthly power). The Kirpan is also one of the 5 K's (see page. 132f). Again there are tremendous possibilities for further study: the area of spiritual power: the importance of the Gurus in Sikhism, the centrality of the Guru Granth Sahib in Sikh worship. Political power: the history of Sikhism and its struggle with the Mughal Empire in its early years. The 5 K's are an area of study for pupils of any age.

Activities

Apart from the areas of study which are outlined above, there are other possibilities:

• The Khanda is emblazened on the Sikh flag which is outside every Gurdwara. Pupils could investigate how the flag pole is ritually cleansed during the festival of Baisakhi.

• See page 137 for other activities relating to the Sikh emblem.

This is just one example of how an artefact could spark off a whole area of study on a particular religion. Other examples for other religions (and this list is not exhaustive) could be:

Christianity: Orthodox burial shroud

Buddhism: wheel of life

Islam: compass

Hinduism: Puja tray

Judaism: tefillin

Jewish artefacts

Contents

Torah

Torah means 'teaching' and is the name of the first five books of the Bible, which contain the basic Jewish laws. These books are the most important of the Jewish Scriptures.

Sefer Torah

A small replica of a Torah Scroll in Western (Ashkenazi) style, 20cm high, with a blue cover.

A small replica of a Torah Scroll in Eastern (Sephardi) style, in a metal case 12cm high.

The Torah is read out in synagogue services from a hand-written parchment scroll (a sefer). It is written in Hebrew, and every scroll is identical apart from its outside cover and decorations. Western scrolls are covered in rich velvet mantles which slip on over the top of the scrolls. Silver crowns or bells are attached to the top of the 2 wooden handles, and a silver breastplate often hangs at the front of the scroll (like the one the high priest used to wear in biblical times). Eastern scrolls are encased in precious metal cases for protection and ornamentation. When not in use, the Torah scroll resides in the Ark, which is a special cabinet at the front of the synagogue (i.e. on the East wall). When a scroll is so old that it can no longer be used, it is buried in a Jewish cemetery because its words are too holy to discard.

Miniature replicas of the Torah scrolls, in both Western and Eastern styles, are produced within the Jewish communities. Jews may buy them as souvenirs from Israel, or to give to a boy to mark his Bar Mitzvah (when he reads from the large Torah scroll at the Sabbath service). They are therefore genuine artefacts for your collection, and useful for pupils to see, since a proper Torah scroll is so valuable that it is out of reach, and would not be given to a non-Jew.

Activities

1 Explore with your pupils the idea of special books. Do they have any books which are very precious to them, and why? How do they treat these books? Are they nicely covered? Do they keep them in a special place? Why do they think Jews bury their old scrolls rather than throwing them away?

2 Find some examples of Hebrew to show your pupils (eg. the British and Foreign Bible Society publishes a Hebrew Bible, and Jewish bookshops sell colourful booklets designed to teach their children Hebrew); and

explain that Hebrew is written from right to left. They may like to write their names in Hebrew (consonants only).

3 Ask your pupils to find out the names and opening words of the first five books of the Bible. (Explain that the Jewish Bible became the Christian Old Testament and that they can look it up therefore in an English Bible; and that the Hebrew name of each book is taken from its opening phrase eg. Genesis would be 'In the beginning')

4 Take your pupils on a visit to a synagogue where they will be able to see a proper Torah Scroll and hear some of the Hebrew being chanted. Make sure they ask about the various decorations they will see on the scrolls.

Yad

Yad means 'hand' and describes the silver pointer which is used when reading from the Torah scroll. Its name comes from the design: a long thin stick ending with a small hand with a pointing finger. It is used so that the reader can keep his place without touching the Torah, which is holy. When not in use, it is hung on the outside of the Torah scroll.

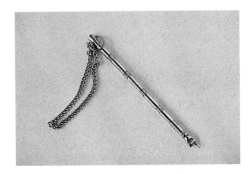

A silver-plated yad or pointer, 19 cm long

Mezuzah

Mezuzah means 'door-post' and it is the name of a tiny scroll which is put into a case and fixed to the door frames of Jewish homes, synagogues

Two Mezuzah cases with Jewish symbols on them. The Hebrew on the larger case, 12cm long, says 'Shaddai' which means 'Almighty' (which is also written on the back of the tiny scroll inside). On the smaller case, 8cm long, just the first letter of 'Shaddai' is used.

and other Jewish buildings. Orthodox Jewish homes will usually have a mezuzah on every room of the house except for the toilet and bathroom.

The scroll contains the first two paragraphs of the *Shema*. The opening of the Shema in Deuteronomy 6: 4-5 sums up the essence of Judaism in these few words:

Hear, O Israel (Shema Yisrael):
The LORD our God, the LORD is One,
and you shall love the LORD your God
with all your heart, and with all your soul,
and with all your might.

The *Shema* goes on to say: 'And you shall write them on the doorposts of your house and on your gates' (v.9), which is the origin of this custom. As Jews go in and out of their homes, they touch the mezuzah and then kiss their fingers. It reminds them of the presence there of the Almighty and that their home is run according to Jewish Law.

NB The mezuzah case is relatively inexpensive, but the scroll for inside it is more expensive. Jews might be unhappy for this scroll to be passed around in class. It may therefore be better to use the empty case in the classroom.

Activities

1 Ask your pupils to write out on a tiny scroll just the first 2 verses of the Shema; and see if they can learn these famous words by heart. Then they can find a little box or make a container to keep it in. This will help them to remember what a *mezuzah* is.

2 Ask your pupils if they have anything on the walls at home which is a special reminder to them of something when they pass it.

3 Ask your pupils to imagine a Jewish family moving into a new house. The father has nailed a beautiful *mezuzah* to the top part of the right-hand doorpost of the front door, with these words (but in Hebrew):

Blessed are You, Lord our God, King of the Universe, who has made us holy with your commandments, commanding us to affix the mezuzah.
Blessed are You, Lord our God, King of the Universe. who has kept us alive and sustained us and permitted us to reach this moment.

Can your pupils imagine how he might feel when he touches the mezuzah, raises his fingers to his lips, and enters his new home?

Israeli flag

The flag of the modern Jewish state of Israel may be seen at a number of Jewish celebrations (eg.amongst the decorations in the sukkah at the festival of Sukkot), but particularly at the festival

of Simchat Torah. The Israeli flag is white with a blue line across the top and bottom, representing the lines on a Jewish prayer-shawl. In the centre is a blue six-pointed star. This is popularly called the Star of David, but in Hebrew it is called the magen David which means 'shield of David'.

Simchat Torah means 'rejoicing in the Torah' and demonstrates the Jewish love for their Scriptures. It is an annual festival which comes on the Sabbath when the end of the Torah Scroll is reached in the synagogue service, and the reader turns to the beginning of the Torah to start the process all over again.   There are joyful processions with the Torah scrolls paraded around the synagogue with singing and dancing. The children march behind waving home-made flags of various designs, either copying the Israeli flag or using other Jewish symbols.

A postcard of the Israeli flag

Activities

1 Ask your pupils to find out who David was, and why his emblem is therefore appropriate on the flag of Israel.

2 Help your pupils to learn to draw the Star of David: they need to see that it is made up of two identical equilateral triangles.

3 Your pupils could make some Israeli flags (either rectangular or triangular).

4 Help your pupils to appreciate something of the Jewish attitude to the Torah. Because they love God, the Jewish laws are not regarded as a burden but as a privilege and Jews are happy to obey them.

Prayer

Jews have set prayers in Hebrew to say at home and in the synagogue. The basic form of Hebrew prayer is the blessing, which expresses thanks to God on many occasions throughout the day, and begins with the words 'Blessed art Thou, O Lord our God, King of the Universe.' Orthodox Jews are also required to pray three times a day: morning, midday and evening.

Siddur

The Authorised Daily Prayer Book, which is used by Orthodox Jews.

Siddur means 'order' and is the name for a Jewish prayer-book because it gives the order of service i.e. it records all the set prayers of the various services.

Phylacteries/ Tefillin

A set of phylacteries and the velvet bag in which they are kept.

A phylactery is a small black leather box attached to leather straps. It contains the same portions of the *Shema* as the *mezuzah* and also passages from Exodus 13. Orthodox Jewish men tie one phylactery to their forehead and another to their upper arm during their weekday prayers, (the alternative name *tefillin* is Hebrew for 'prayers'). This is in fulfilment of the command: 'And you shall bind them as a sign upon your hand, and they shall be as frontlets between your eyes' (Deuteronomy 6:8).

A set of phylacteries costs over £100 and are therefore unlikely to be found in school artefact collections; but you may be able to borrow them from an RE Centre. The CEM video *Judaism through the eyes of Jewish children* shows how they are worn. As with mezuzah scrolls, Jews may be unhappy about these being passed round in class.

Activities

Can your pupils suggest any significance for Jewish worshippers in binding these boxes containing the Shema to their foreheads and near their hearts?

Tallit

A linen tallit 160cm x 30cm. It is white with blue and gold stripes.

The *tallit* is a prayer shawl worn by Jewish males over the age of 13 (and is therefore a suitable *Bar Mitzvah* present). It is wrapped around the shoulders or over the head during prayer, and expresses the belief that God is all around us. It comes in various sizes, the most popular being 150cm by 60cm. The shawl is white or cream with black or blue stripes at each end. The long fringes (called *tzitzith*) in the four corners are essential, and fulfil the commandment in Numbers 15:37-41. In that passage it explains that these fringes are reminders of the commandments.

Activities

This could be part of a study of special clothes, or clothes worn for religious services. Introduce the study with younger children by getting them to cut out pictures of clothes worn for special reasons (eg. a mackintosh to keep dry, an overall to keep clean, a space outfit, uniforms of various organisations, party clothes etc.)

Skull cap

The Jewish skull cap is called a kippah, capel or yarmulka.   Some Jewish men wear one all the time to remind them that God is above them. Others only wear them as prayer-caps during services, because Jews must cover their heads when they pray, as a sign of respect to God.

Men are usually asked to cover their heads when entering a synagogue or other Jewish holy places, and often cardboard or paper skull-caps are provided for visitors.

A satin and a velvet skull cap.

Activities

Your pupils might like to make a Jewish skull cap from material or sugar paper (see diagram), decorating it with Jewish symbols if they wish.

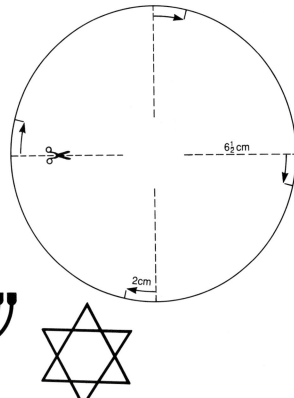

Cut out a circle of sugar-paper 8cm radius. Mark out the lines to be cut along, as shown, and cut them. Take each cut edge across to the 2cm mark, and staple.

Each of the four sides can be decorated with a Jewish symbol.

$6\frac{1}{2}$ cm

2cm

Bar/Bat Mitzvah

The age of majority in Judaism is 12 for a girl and 13 for a boy. At this age they are considered a *bat mitzvah* ('daughter of the commandment') or *bar mitzvah* ('son of the commandment').

In Orthodox synagogues it has been the custom to celebrate a boy's *bar mitzvah* on the Sabbath nearest to his 13th birthday, when he takes his place among the men of the synagogue and may take a part in leading the service (it is traditional

for him to read from the Torah on that day). He will prepare for this day several years beforehand, being instructed in the rules of his religion, and learning to read the Hebrew of the set passage from the Torah. There is usually a party during the following week.

In Reform and Liberal Synagogues, the girls also have special rituals to mark their *bat mitzvoth* (plural of *mitzvah*).

Bar/Bat Mitzvah cards

A selection of cards for Bar Mitzvah and Bat Mitzvah

There are many designs of cards available. Boys and girls receive many cards and presents on this special day of theirs.

Activities

1 Divide older pupils into small groups. Give each group a Bar or Bat Mitzvah card and ask them to say all they can about coming of age in Judaism from the pictures and greetings on the card.

2 Set older pupils the task of finding out what celebrations there may be for a girl on her bat mitzvah.

Sabbath

The Sabbath (*Shabbat*) is the best day of the week for Jews. It is a holy day, a day of rest and a day for the family to enjoy being together. It lasts from Friday evening to Saturday night.

Festival candles

A festival candlestick.

On Friday evenings the mother lights the white festive candles, reciting a blessing. If there is no woman present, then someone else will light them. There must be at least two candles; and in some families there are as many candles as there are children.

These candles are also lit at the beginning of every other holy day, and not just on the Sabbath. The candlesticks are often made of precious metal, like silver, and may be family heirlooms. They are a traditional present for a girl on reaching her *bat mitzvah*, as she looks forward to her responsibility in the Jewish home.

Activities

1 Ask pupils why they think candles are lit at times of celebration. What other examples can they think of?

2 Pupils could write out this translation of the Jewish blessing which is said in Hebrew over the lighted candles:

Blessed are You, Lord our God, King of the Universe.
You make us holy with your commandments;
and you command us to light the candles for Sabbath.

This could be decorated in an appropriate way, and perhaps mounted on a large cut-out shape of candlesticks.

Challah loaves

Two plaited challah loaves.

On the Sabbath, and at other Jewish festivals, the meal begins with blessings said over wine and two loaves of bread, which are then shared round with everyone present. The bread is of a special kind. It is rich, challah bread, made by adding eggs and by plaiting the dough. It is important that there are two loaves. This recalls the biblical Period in the Wilderness when the Jews lived on manna and had to collect two portions the day before the Sabbath because this was a day of rest.

Activities

1 Buy two *challah* loaves (some large supermarkets stock them on Thursdays and Fridays). Let your pupils taste the special cake-like texture of this bread.

2 Buy two *challah* loaves. Varnish them with clear varnish, being careful to cover them completely so that they are air-tight. They should now last for permanent display, but must not be eaten!

3 Find a recipe in a Jewish cookery book or text-book and arrange for pupils to bake some *challah* bread.

Challah cover

The Sabbath loaves are always covered, often with a beautifully embroidered cloth. It is said that the bread must be covered while the wine is blessed first, to prevent it from getting jealous! The covers are often decorated with symbols of the Sabbath such as candlesticks, wine and plaited loaves.

A cover for the challah loaves, with the Hebrew for 'Shabbat' on it.

Activities

Your pupils may like to make a challah cover. The cloth is usually square (side about 36 cm), with Sabbath symbols embroidered or painted on it using suitable paint. A fringe may be sewn round the edge for decoration.

Havdalah

At the end of the Sabbath, the family gathers round for the Havdalah ceremony. This short service 'distinguishes' the Sabbath from the rest of the working week. It is a final opportunity to remember the sights, tastes and smells of the Sabbath.

Wine goblet and saucer

A wine goblet and saucer.

The wine is poured to overflow the goblet, into the saucer, as a sign of God's abundant goodness. A blessing is said over it and it is shared with those present.

Any wine glass/goblet and saucer may be used, although you can get silver sets.

Havdalah candle and holder

A Havdalah candle (26cm high) in a special candle-holder.

Next, the special Havdalah candle is lit. This is made from two thin candles, with wicks at either end, folded and woven together, so that there are four wicks to light. This makes sense of the blessing which is said over the Havdalah candle, which speaks of 'lights' in the plural. It is usually held by a child and finally extinguished in the wine in the saucer. The fact that lights are kindled shows that the Sabbath is over, since this work is forbidden on the Sabbath.

Havdalah candles are sometimes all one colour (eg. white or yellow), or two colours (eg. blue and white). They may be held on their own or in a candle-holder specially designed for its shape.

Spice box

An olive-wood spice box 17cm high, from Israel, with the the Star of David (the 'Magen David', literally 'the shield of David') on it, and also the 'menorah' (the seven-branched candlestick).

Havdalah spice boxes may be wooden, like the one shown, or they may be ornate silver versions, which are often given as a traditional wedding present. They usually have Jewish symbols on them. The lid lifts off to reveal a small recepticle for spices. When it is replaced, the perfume of the spices can be smelt through the holes in the lid. (It is a good idea to keep cloves in here for classroom use, as these will not make a mess if they spill out.)

A blessing is said over the spices, and the box is passed round for everyone to smell them. In this way, the sweet fragrance of the Sabbath lingers with them into the following week.

Activities

Make a class collection of different types of spices. Each pupil could make a spice box (of any shape), with holes in the lid.
Pass round the boxes with different spices in them, and ask pupils to write down as many words as possible to describe their fragrances.

Passover

Passover (*Pesach*) is the most important annual festival of the Jews. It is a Spring festival which lasts 8 days. It commemorates the Exodus of the Jews from slavery in Egypt, under the leadership of their great Prophet and Law-giver, Moses.

Seder Plate

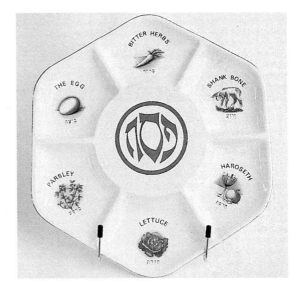

A Seder plate with the Hebrew for 'Pesach' in the centre.

The Passover celebrations begin in the evening with the Seder service which follows a set 'order'. This takes place at the family meal-table where symbolic foods are used to tell the story of the Exodus, before a proper meal is eaten. A special Seder plate may be used for the six symbolic foods:

charoset - an apple mixture which reminds them of the mortar with which the Jewish slaves built cities for Pharaoh;

bitter herbs - usually horseradish, to remind them of the bitterness of slavery;

lettuce - which tastes pleasant at first but leaves a bitter taste in the mouth, like the experience of the Jews in Egypt;

shank bone - to remind them of the roast lamb which they ate before leaving;

parsley - which reminds them of the branches with which they daubed their doorposts with the blood of the lambs;

roasted egg - for the new life they escaped to.

There is also a dish of salt water, representing the tears of the Jewish slaves.

Activities

1 Set up a *Seder* plate and use it to tell the story of the Exodus. If you have not got a proper *Seder* plate it is quite acceptable to use just a large plate or a set of ramekin dishes.

2 Young pupils could colour and cut out pictures of the six symbolic foods, and stick them onto paper plates for display.

3 See how many explanations your pupils can find of the *Seder* foods (there are both some alternative foods and explanations to the ones given above).

4 Older pupils could make a chart of the *Seder* foods with their symbolic meanings explained.

Matzah

A box of matzos which is 'kosher' or fit for use at Passover, and two individual matzos.

Before Passover begins the house is Spring-cleaned and all traces of leaven are removed. Only the flat, unleavened bread is allowed to be eaten during the week of Passover. It reminds the Jews of how their ancestors fled from Egypt without having time for the bread to rise.

Freshly baked *matzos* (or *matzoth*) are usually oval in shape; but these boxes of rectangular *matzos* are very popular, and Jewish families buy sufficient to last them throughout the 8 days of Passover. Jews have devised ingenious ways of using *matzos* and *matzah* flour for all sorts of recipes during the Passover week.

Activities

Buy a box of matzos from a large supermarket, and let your pupils taste some. (Be prepared for a lot of crumbs, because they are like highly baked water-biscuits.)

Matzah cover

During the Seder service three matzos are used, and are kept in a special cover with three sections to it. The top and bottom matzos are instead of the festive *challah* loaves. The middle piece is called 'the bread of affliction' and represents the unleavened bread of the Exodus story. This piece is broken in two by the leader of the *Seder* and the first half is eaten during the service. The other half, the *Afikomen* ('dessert') is hidden, and the children search for it at the end of the first part of the service and bargain with it because the second half of the *Seder* service cannot begin without it.

A matzah cover with a picture of the symbolic Seder foods on it.

Activities

Your pupils may wish to make a matzah cover. They will need four squares of cloth (side about 26 cm long) placed on top of each other. The top square should be decorated in some way with Jewish symbols. One side of each square should be hemmed (this will be the side that is left open). Then all four squares should be sewn together on the other three sides: either using blanket-stitch to stop fraying and to make an attractive finish; or using bias-binding to cover up the rough edges.

Haggadah

A Haggadah in Hebrew and English.

The *Haggadah* is the service book used for the Seder service. Its name means 'telling' because it tells the story of the Exodus. The service is in Hebrew, but these booklets often contain translations in the everyday language. You can find attractive children's versions, some with pop-up or moving pictures.

Chanukah

Chanukah is the Jewish winter festival of light which comes in November or December. Chanukah means 'dedication' because this festival commemorates the rededication of the Temple in Jerusalem after it had been recaptured from the Syrian oppressors in the 2nd century BCE. The story of this Jewish rebellion and the cleansing of the Temple can be read in the Books of I and II Maccabees in the Apocrypha.

Chanukiyyah

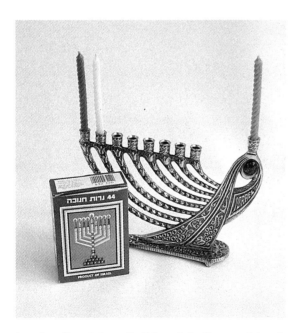

A modern Chanukah candlestick ready for the second day of the festival. It has the emblems of the 12 Tribes of Israel on it, and the servant candle on the top. A box of Chanukah candles (10 cm high) stands beside it with a picture of a more traditionally shaped chanukiyyah on it.

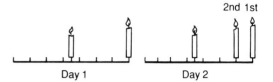

Day 1   Day 2

The festival of Chanukah lasts for 8 days and is celebrated by burning one candle on the first evening, two on the second and so on until all eight candles are lit on the final day. The candles are lit after dark and must be allowed to burn right down, with new candles used each day. The diagram shows the order in which they are lit.

The special candlestick used is called a chanukiyyah. It can be of any design but ought to have the eight candles on the same level in a room. There is often a ninth candle-holder, apart from the rest, for the *shamash* or 'servant' candle with which the others are lit.

The lighting of a candelabrum recalls a miraculous event which is said to have taken place when the Temple was rededicated. There was only a day's supply left of the purest olive oil which was used to light the Temple's great seven-branched candlestick (the *menorah*). Yet, although it took eight days to get fresh supplies, the *menorah* kept burning.

Activities

1 Your pupils may like to make a *chanukiyyah* eg. with clay; with plastic bottle lids set in plasticine; or even with 8 upturned clay flower-pots with

C-H-A-N-U-K-A-H painted on them.

2 See if your pupils can work out why *Chanukah* candles come in boxes of 44.

3 Many *Chanukah* candlesticks have symbols on them which are worth exploring and will help your pupils to consolidate their knowledge of Judaism.

Dreidel

Four small plastic dreidels with Hebrew letters on each side.

It is traditional for children to play a special game at Chanukah using a *dreidel* (a small four-sided spinning top) and counters. On each side of the dreidel is a Hebrew letter which begins one of the four Hebrew words for 'A great - miracle - happened -there (or here)'. These letters have the following values:

ב Do nothing

ג Take all the kitty

ה Take half the kitty

ש (or פ) Put a counter in the kitty

The counters are divided equally at the start of the game and each player puts one counter in the kitty. The first player spins the dreidel and when it falls he reads off the letter on top. which means that he either gets nothing or adds or takes from the kitty. Before the next player spins, each person puts another counter in the kitty (or this could be done when there are no counters left or only one remains in the kitty). This continues until the winner has all the counters.

Activities

1 'A great miracle happened there.' Tell your pupils the story of the miracle of the oil, and of the deliverance of the Jews from the power of the mighty Syrian empire. They may wish to dramatise it.

2 Your pupils could make simple cardboard dreidels and play the Chanukah game. They will need a small square of stiff cardboard (marked off by pen, as in the diagram) and a cocktail stick pushed through the centre point to spin it with.

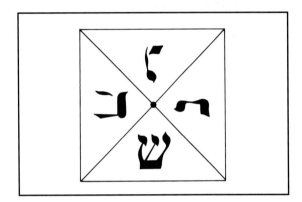

Chanukah cards

A selection of Chanukah cards, showing aspects of this festival.

Chanukah cards are popular in the United States but are not readily available in this country. Like all Jewish cards, they will probably have some Hebrew on them and therefore may open from right to left.

Activities

Since this festival is particularly popular with children, your pupils might like to make some Chanukah cards for children, with pictures connected with Chanukah and an appropriate greeting for this festival of light.

Chanukah foods

Fried potato latkes made from grated potatoes and onions mixed with eggs and flour.

Because of the miracle of the oil, it is traditional at Chanukah time to eat foods cooked in oil, such as doughnuts and potato *latkes*.

Activities

If you have the facilities, make some potato latkes with your class. They should be eaten hot.

Rosh Hashanah

Rosh Hashanah, which comes in September or October, is the Jewish New Year.

Shofar

A small ram's horn.

A shofar is a trumpet usually made from a ram's horn (although it may be made from the horn of any animal considered clean by Jewish law). On *Rosh Hashanah* the ram's horn is blown repeatedly in the synagogue, in accordance with Numbers 29:1. It is a call to conscience (*Hashanah* or 'Hosanna' means 'Save us now.') Although New Year is a time of celebration, it is also the beginning of the Ten Days of Penitence which ends on Yom Kippur, the Day of Atonement. (The Shofar is blown once at the end of Yom Kippur.) So this is a solemn period for the Jews, when they put behind them their failings and look to the year ahead with a fresh determination to do God's will.

Activities

The shofar is a call to conscience. Discuss with pupils the sort of things that can prick our consciences (eg. television pictures of starving children in the Third World, or more personal examples). Ask if they think it is good to have a conscience? Can we have an overactive conscience?

Rosh Hashanah foods

An apple and a honey pot for Rosh Hashanah.

It is traditional at *Rosh Hashanah* to eat slices of apple dipped in honey. This is to wish each other a sweet/happy New year. Some Jews also make bread for the festival in special shapes. A round crusty loaf, for instance, hopes that the coming year will be just perfect (since a circle is complete and whole, a perfect shape).

Activities

1 Ask your pupils what they would want to wish for their friends, their families and themselves at New Year. What foods would express these wishes?

2 The circle is used as a symbol in many religions and cultures. How many examples can your pupils think of?

New Year cards

A selection of Rosh Hashanah cards.

Rosh Hashanah is the main festival for Jews to send each other annual greetings, and these cards can often be bought in large high-street card shops. They usually have Jewish symbols on them, especially those symbols to do with *Rosh Hashanah*. They may have Hebrew on them and may therefore open from right to left, since Hebrew is written from the right.

Activities

1 Get a selection of *Rosh Hashan*ah cards for your pupils to look through. Ask them to copy out the greetings (the same formula often recurs), to see what kind of things Jews wish each other at New Year.

2 After studying *Rosh Hashanah*, ask your pupils to make a card for this festival with an appropriate picture and message on it. String the cards across the classroom to make a colourful display.

Sukkot

Sukkot (or Tabernacles)is an Autumn festival. Its name comes from the *sukkah* which Jews are commanded to live in during this week. A *sukkah* is a makeshift dwelling and recalls both the Jewish wanderings in the Wilderness after the Exodus; and also the fruit harvest in Israel during which the Jews lived in little huts in their vineyards and olive groves. By eating meals, and perhaps sleeping, out in a *sukkah*, Jews are reminded of their dependence on God the Creator.

Arba Minim

A palm branch and special holder produced for Sukkot to hold together the three types of branches which are required.

The *Arba Minim* are the Four Species of plant used in services at *Sukkot*. They are a *lulav* or palm branch, three myrtle branches, 2 willow branches and an *etrog* or 'citron' (which looks like a large lemon). They are signs of God's abundant provision at this harvest festival, but they also have more specific symbolic meanings.

One interpretation is that the palm branch is tall and straight like the backbone; the myrtle's leaves are the shape of eyes; the willow's leaves are like lips; and the citron is the shape of a heart. They stand for different human characteristics: someone who is brave and strong; someone who sees good in others; someone who speaks with knowledge and understanding of the Torah; someone who is loving and compassionate.

The *Arba Minim* are specially imported from Israel, and each Jewish family tries to buy one (and in 1990 they cost from about £25.00 !).

Activities

1 See if young pupils can identify the Four Species with the four parts of the body. See if older pupils can find out other interpretations Jews give to the Four Species.

2 If you are studying Sukkot in the first half of the Autumn term, contact a synagogue and ask if you may borrow the Arba Minim to show your pupils. (Unfortunately, the only parts of this which can be kept as permanent artefacts are those shown in the photograph).

Purim

Purim is a Spring festival in which the biblical story of Esther is recalled. This story is set in the 6th century BCE when the Holy Land belonged to the Persian Empire. It tells how Esther, the Jewish queen of the great Persian king, bravely saved her people from annihilation. The festival is a time of great revelry, and there are fancy-dress parades with the carnival queen as Esther.

Megillah

An inexpensive printed 'megillah' of the Book of Esther, 15 cm high.

Although we normally think of the Torah when we talk of Jewish scrolls, there are in fact five other books of the Bible which are produced on individual scrolls and read on special occasions (Song of Songs, Ruth, Lamentations, Ecclesiastes and Esther).

Purim is such a popular festival that most Jews have their own printed copy of the *megillah* which is read in Hebrew in the synagogue on that day. Often these copies include illustrations of the story.

Activities

1 Read through to yourself the Book of Esther in the Bible or a summary of the story from a textbook on Judaism. Then tell the story to your class. This could be done with the use of puppets for younger children (you may be able to buy some genuine Purim puppets in Jewish shops early in the year).

2 Ask your pupils to make their own megillah. They could write the story of Esther in columns, starting at the right hand side of the strip of paper, and roll up the scroll onto one handle as seen in the photograph. If they prefer, they could do a picture-strip of the story on the scroll.

Gregger

A *gregger* is like a football-rattle, used to make a noise during the reading of the story of Esther in the synagogue. Esther and her cousin Mordecai were the heroes of the story, but Haman was the 'baddy'. He was King Ahasuerus' chief minister who plotted the destruction of the Jews, but ended up being executed. So whenever Haman's name is mentioned, the synagogue erupts into boos, hisses and the loud noise of the *greggers*. People write 'Haman' in chalk on the soles of their shoes, and stamp their feet to blot out his name. There are also special three-cornered cakes for Purim which are known as 'Haman's ears' or 'Haman's pockets'.

A wooden gregger used at Purim.

Activities

1 Your pupils could make their own rattles using two small paper plates stapled together on a stick with dried beans inside. The plates could be painted with the faces of characters in the story.

2 One group could act out the story of Purim, and the rest of the class could join in with cheers or rattles, in pantomime fashion.

Christian artefacts

Contents

Teachings

Christians believe in God the Holy Trinity: Father, Son and Holy Spirit. God's guidance is sought mainly through the Bible and the Church.

The Bible

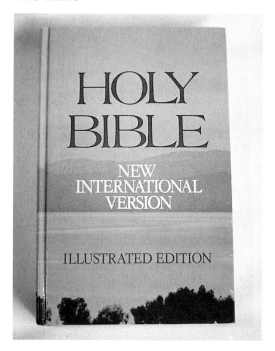

A Modern English version of the Bible.

The Bible is the Christian Holy book. It has two main parts; the Old Testament (which is the Jewish Bible) and the New Testament. The New Testament is the most important part for Christians, and is often printed separately. The New Testament contains the four Gospels, which tell the 'Good News' of the ministry of Jesus Christ; the history of the early church; and the teachings of the early Christian leaders, mostly preserved in letters to the churches.

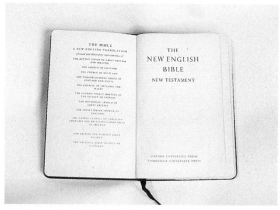

A pocket edition of the New Testament.

The Bible was originally written in Hebrew and Greek, but Christians read it in their own languages, and there are many English versions available.

Christians believe that God speaks to them through these Scriptures because they are the inspired Word of God. They read, study and meditate upon the Bible to help them work out what to believe and how to live their lives. They may study the Bible with the help of scholarly books called Commentaries which 'comment' in detail on each word of the text; or they may use booklets which set them a passage to read each day with some ideas to think and pray about.

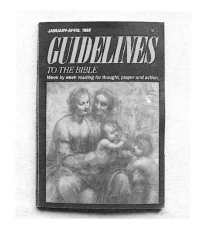

Bible study notes

Activities

1 Help your pupils to become familiar with handling the Bible and finding their way around it. Start with the division of the Bible into the two Testaments. With older pupils, call out references from the Gospels, and see who can find them first.

2 Ask your pupils to count up how many books there are in the Old and the New Testaments, to help them appreciate that the Bible is really a large collection of books rather than just one or two books.

3 Your class could make little book covers with folded pieces of sugar-paper and write on the cover of each the name of a book in the Bible. These could be displayed under the titles 'Old Testament' and 'New Testament'.

4 A Bible bookshelf could be made with matchboxes for the books of the Bible (39 for the Old Testament or 46 in a Catholic version, and 27 for the New Testament). Each box should be covered, with the name of a biblical book written down the 'spine'. A cardboard box could be converted into a bookshelf to hold the books. The index of some Bibles will help you to divide the books into groups eg. Pentateuch, History, Poetry, Prophets, Gospels, Acts, Letters, Prophecy.

despite the fact that many schools and churches are now abandoning the hymn book for the overhead projector.

Hymn Books

Hymns are religious songs which express Christian beliefs. They form an important part of the services in many Churches. Hymns are deeply embedded in our Christian culture, as can be seen from the popularity of such programmes as the long-running *Songs of Praise* on television. If your school uses hymns or songs in assembly,.then your pupils will readily understand the purpose of a hymn-book,

Activities

1 Younger children might simply enjoy singing some hymns, particularly those they use in school assemblies.

2 Older pupils might be able to get a feel of the different church traditions from a range of hymn books.

3 Hymns can also be studied for Christian teachings e.g. the hymns for Holy Week and Easter.

Advent

Advent is celebrated in Roman Catholic and Anglican Churches. It is the period in the Church's year of about a month leading up to Christmas. It begins on the Sunday nearest to St.Andrew's Day which comes on 30th November, and finishes on 24th December, the day before Christmas. The word 'advent' comes from the Latin for 'coming' or 'arrival', and is the time when Christians prepare to celebrate the birth of Jesus at Christmas. The Church also reminds Christians at this time of its belief in the Second Coming of Christ in triumph to judge the world.

Advent candle

This is a large white candle, 30 cm. high, which takes about half an hour to burn down from one number to the next. The pictures on it are religious nativity scenes, but Advent candles might have any Christmas, seasonal or Christian transfers on them.

Advent candles are marked off with 24 numbers, despite the fact that the length of Advent varies slightly from year to year. They are intended to be used from the beginning of December, with the candle burnt down one number each day until December 24th, when the candle should be completely used up. They are a means of counting off the days before Christmas.

Activities

1 Ask your pupils to find out the date of Advent Sunday (from a diary or by finding the nearest Sunday to 30th November); and to count up how many days there are in Advent this year.

2 Make a large Advent candle from cardboard, to fix on the classroom wall. Mark off sections for the number of days in Advent. Colour in a section of it each day from the beginning of Advent until the end of term, to help young children count off the days to Christmas. See if they can think of something different each day that people do to prepare for Christmas, and make a list.

3 Buy an Advent candle for your class, and burn it down at a special time each day (perhaps to create a quiet, thoughtful time at the beginning or end of the day). Give your pupils a chance to record their thoughts and feelings in poetry.

NB Be careful to observe fire regulations eg. embed the candle in a tray of sand, on a firm surface, away from the children so that their hair or clothes cannot brush against the flame.

Advent wreath

An Advent wreath

An Advent wreath is a circle of evergreen (eg. holly) with four small candles placed equidistant around the circle and a large white candle in the middle. The small candles are often red, or they may be purple which is the liturgical colour for Advent.

The four candles represent the four Sundays during Advent. On the first Sunday of Advent, one small candle is lit during the Church service. On the next Sunday, two are lit, and so on. On Christmas day the central candle is also lit, to celebrate the birth of Jesus, the Light of the world.

In cathedrals, where services are held every day,there may be a large Advent ring with a candle for every day during Advent.

Activities

1 Ask a group of pupils to make an Advent wreath for display, starting with a circle of plasticine on a board, to push the candles and holly into. If you want to keep it from one year to the next, use plastic holly leaves.

2 Explore with your pupils why light is a particularly important symbol for Advent. Younger children can respond to the idea of light brightening up the dark days of winter and of anticipating Christmas celebrations. Older pupils could look up John 8:12 and the Anglican collect for the First Sunday in Advent, to see how the symbol is used for the coming of Jesus into the world and the victory of good over evil.

Advent calendar

An Advent calendar, like an Advent candle, assumes mistakenly that Advent always starts on 1st December. It has 24 windows, one to be opened each day leading up to Christmas. Inside each window is a picture to do with Christmas, a short verse from the Bible, or a small piece of chocolate. Traditional Advent calendars have the Nativity scene on them, but there are many modern secular alternatives.

An Advent calendar with Christmas nativity scenes on it

Activities

1 Ask your pupils to design and make a large Advent calendar. They will need to paint a Christmas picture on a large piece of card, then draw on it 24 numbered windows which are cut around three of their sides so that they can be opened. This should be stuck onto another piece of card of the same size, and 24 small pictures stuck in place under the windows (they could be 24 Christmas symbols cut out of old Christmas cards). Ask your pupils to explain why these symbols are connected with Christmas. When finished, the calendar should be put on display and a window opened each day during Advent.

Christmas

Christmas commemorates the birth of Jesus Christ and is the most popular Christian festival, particularly with children. It is celebrated with Christmas dinner, parties and the exchange of cards and presents. Churches hold special services when carols are sung and a Nativity Play may be performed. The service of Midnight Mass on Christmas Eve is especially popular in Catholic and Anglican Churches.

The Christmas season continues in the Church from 25th December until Epiphany on 6th January, which commemorates the 'revelation' of Jesus as the Christ to the Wise Men and, later in life, his revelation at his adult baptism by John in the River Jordan.

Christingle

A Christingle is an orange, with a small candle pushed into the top with four cocktail sticks full of nuts and raisins, and a red ribbon tied round the middle. The orange represents the world, the four sticks stand for the corners of the world (or the four seasons), with the fruits of the earth on them. The red ribbon stands for the blood of Christ, and the candle for Jesus the Light of the World.

The idea originated in America and was popularised in this country by the Children's Society which held its first Christingle service in Lincoln Cathedral in 1968. Many churches now

A Christingle

Christmas symbols, like the yule log, and to find out their origins and meanings. Then ask them to create their own, new symbol for Christmas.

Christmas crib

A hand-made crib with rough pottery figures.

hold Christingle services in the week before Christmas. They are especially popular with children who each hold a Christingle which lights up the darkened church.

<hr>

Activities

1 Your pupils could make their own Christingles and learn about their symbolic meaning. (If you want one to keep in your artefact collection, it could be made with a plastic orange and with small pieces of plasticine on the sticks.)

2 Young pupils could think of as many words as possible to describe light (eg. sparkling, shining, glittering). Each word could be written on yellow, orange or red sugar-paper cut into the shape of a flame, and used for display.

3 This Christmas symbol has only become popular comparatively recently. Ask your pupils to think of other

A Christmas crib is a model of the stable where Jesus was born, with animals and figures of Mary, Joseph and the baby Jesus, the shepherds and sometimes also the Wise Men who came to worship Jesus. Many churches have a Christmas crib on display during Christmas; and a short ceremony to bless the crib takes place on Christmas Eve. This is sometimes a special service for children during the afternoon before Christmas, or it may take place at the beginning of Midnight Mass. Many Christians also have little models in their homes as part of their Christmas decorations.

This custom originated with St.Francis who, in 1223, converted a cave into a Christmas nativity scene with a real manger and animals, and held Midnight Mass there for the villagers.

Activities

1 Make a Christmas crib with your class, with different groups making the different models: a stable or cave; an ox and an ass; a manger with the baby Jesus in it; Mary; Joseph; shepherds and some sheep. Use it to tell the Christmas story found in Luke 2:1-20.

Christmas cards

There are many varieties of greetings cards which people send each other at Christmas. Some have religious pictures and messages, but many are secular.

A selection of Christmas cards

Activities

Collect old Christmas cards at the beginning of the Spring term and use these in your RE lessons in the following ways:

1 Your pupils could select those pictures which they think have a religious message (this could include aspects of celebration like food and parties, since Christians celebrate the birthday of Jesus). Younger pupils, working together, could be asked to sort a selection of cards into two groups: 'The Jesus story' and 'not the Jesus story'. A third category of 'don't know's' might emerge, which could then be discussed with the whole class.

2 Older pupils could find those with Nativity scenes and decide whether they fit with the story in Matthew's or Luke's Gospel (or both). They should consider what these two writers were trying to say about Jesus with their different emphases: Jesus born as an outcast in a stable and visited by poor shepherds; Jesus adored by wise men with their rich gifts.

3 They could make a collection of the different greetings inside the cards and discuss in groups which they prefer and why.

4 Ask each pupil to make a Christmas card for someone special with their own greetings or verse inside it. (It could be to give to some old people that your school entertains or gives parcels to at Christmas time.)

Christmas books

A selection of children's books to do with Christmas

There are many books available to do with Christmas, many of which are for children, covering Christmas carols, Nativity stories and others, Christmas customs and activity books.

Easter

Easter is the most important Christian festival, celebrating as it does the death and resurrection of Jesus Christ. Many Churches keep the period of six weeks before Easter, called Lent, as a special time of preparation. The last week of Lent is known as Holy Week, when the final events in Jesus' life are remembered, especially his institution of Holy Communion on Maundy Thursday and his death on Good Friday. Easter Sunday is a time of great rejoicing (and has led to Sunday being the Christian holy day each week - the day of Resurrection).

The Easter season continues for 40 days until Ascension Day which celebrates the Christian belief that Jesus 'ascended' into heaven to reign with God the Father in glory. Ten days later comes Whit Sunday which celebrates the coming of the Holy Spirit.

Pancakes

A pancake is a religious artefact which can be quickly prepared and equally quickly eaten up! Its religious significance is that Christians would use up all their rich foods like eggs and butter on the Tuesday before Lent started, because Lent was traditionally a time of fasting. The custom of eating pancakes and having pancake-races on this day is still very popular, although fasting has gone out of fashion for many Christians. The day is called Shrove Tuesday, from the word to be 'shriven' or forgiven of your sins. Some Christians go to confession on this day in preparation for the solemn period of Lent.

Activities

1 If the facilities are available, find a recipe and help your pupils to cook enough pancakes for each of them to have a piece. Make sure they know the reasons for eating pancakes on Shrove Tuesday.

2 Each class could put forward a contender for a school pancake-race. (A thick, leathery pancake is not so appetising but is less likely to fall to pieces when tossed, and a light-weight frying-pan is easier to run with.) Use this event to draw attention to the religious significance of pancakes, in the school assembly.

Holy Week service books

The book in the photograph is from the Anglican Church. *This is Holy Week* contains a selection of prayers and readings which can be used in services. *This is Holy Week* explains the various rituals which may be used. Such books provide useful information for teachers as well as being an addition to your artefact collection.

Stations of the Cross

In the Middle Ages it became popular to go on pilgrimage to religious sites, and various rituals became associated with them. In Jerusalem, pilgrims followed the stages of Jesus' journey to his crucifixion and burial; and there are plaques in the Via Dolorosa there (meaning 'Way of Sorrows') marking these 'Stations of the Cross.' Most Christians never visit the Holy Land, and so the custom developed, particularly among Roman catholics, of placing 14 plaques showing the Stations of the Cross on the walls inside their churches. During Holy Week Christians use them to make their own token pilgrimage. They move from one Station to the next, reading appropriate passages from the Bible and meditating on its personal significance for them.

The 14 Stations of the Cross are as follows (there is a growing custom these days to add a 15th - the Resurrection):

(i)   Jesus is condemned to death

(ii)   Jesus receives the cross

(iii)   Jesus falls the first time

(iv)   Jesus is met by Mary his mother

(v)   The cross is laid on Simon of Cyrene

(vi)   Veronica wipes the face of Jesus

(vii) Jesus falls the second time

(viii) The women of Jerusalem mourn for Jesus

(ix)   Jesus falls a third time

(x)   Jesus is stripped of his clothes

(xi)   Jesus is nailed to the cross

(xii) Jesus dies on the cross

(xiii) Jesus is taken down from the cross

(xiv) Jesus is placed in the tomb

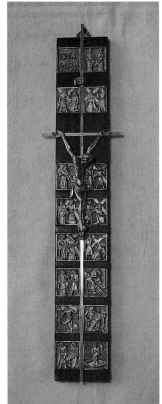

The Stations of the Cross, set around a crucifix.

A selection of booklets helping children and
adults to meditate on the Stations of the Cross.

Activities

1 Take older pupils on a visit to a Catholic church, or an
Anglican church which has the Stations of the Cross, and
ask the priest there to explain how they are used. Give
your pupils a list of the 14 Stations so that they can
identify each one more easily.

2 If you feel it is appropriate to the age of your pupils,
obtain pictures of the Stations of the Cross to be displayed
in your classroom. Posters can be bought at some
catholic bookshops; or you or a pupil could take a set of
photographs in a local church; or your pupils could make
their own (eg. drawing, paintings, collage, clay plaques),
perhaps adding a 15th one on the Resurrection.

3 Buy some Catholic booklets on the Way of the Cross,
particularly the easier ones written for children, so that
your pupils can find out how the Stations can have
significance for Christians today.

The Cross

Because Jesus was crucified, the cross has
become the main Christian symbol, reminding
Christians of his sacrifice for them and his victory
over death. The cross is found in many places
(eg. the traditional shape of a church building is
cruciform) and in many designs. Below are
some of the most common, with their meanings.

The plain Latin cross

This empty cross reminds
Christians that Jesus Christ
conquered death. This
simple cross, often made
of wood, can be seen in
Protestant churches.

Examples of crosses.

An Eastern Orthodox cross with icons on it

A cross mounted on three steps

The steps represent faith, hope and love: the three main Christian virtues (as in 1 Corinthians 13), and represent a Christian coming to Jesus Christ.

A crucifix

A crucifix is a cross with the figure of Jesus on it, usually portraying the agony of his death. It may have the title 'INRI' at the top of it, the first letters of the Latin for: Jesus of Nazareth King of the Jews. Crucifixes are particularly popular in Roman Catholic and Orthodox Churches.

Christ the King

Another traditional type of cross has the figure of Jesus on it robed and portrayed as a glorious king. This reflects the teaching in John's Gospel which sees Jesus as being lifted up on the cross in triumph (see John 12:31-32).

Russian Orthodox Cross

This traditional Russian cross has three cross-beams on it: the top one for the title nailed to the cross to publicise Jesus' crime; the main beam to which his arms were fixed; and a bar for his feet so that he could support the weight of his body.

St.Andrew's Cross

The connection of this cross with St.Andrew can only be traced back as far as the 14th century. Although it looks like our letter X, it is also in the shape of the Greek letter 'chi' which begins the word 'Christ', and this is its special religious significance.

The Greek Cross

This became the emblem of St.George as a red cross on a white background.

The Maltese Cross

This has eight points to represent the eight blessings recorded in the Beatitudes (Matthew 5:1-12). It has been adopted as the emblem of the Saint John Ambulance Brigade.

Palm Cross

It is traditional in Churches which celebrate Palm Sunday, to make small crosses from dried palm leaves from the Holy Land and to distribute them to the worshippers after the crosses have been blessed. Many Christians have their palm cross on display during Holy Week, and some Christians keep them afterwards in their Bibles as book marks. It reminds them of the events of Holy Week and the fickleness of human nature. Palm Sunday commemorates Jesus' triumphal entry into Jerusalem, when people waved palm branches in welcome; but by Friday the cheers of the people had turned to cries to have him crucified.

Activities

1 See how many examples of crosses you can collect with your class, and find out what special significance is in their shape.

2 See how many other symbols your pupils can find combined with crosses, and help them to find out what these symbols mean. A traditional one, for instance, is the Celtic Cross which has a circle on it. Can your pupils guess what a circle represents here? (The same symbolism of something never ending is in the wedding ring)

3 Give your pupils photo-copied outlines of the Union Flag (called the Union Jack when flown from a ship's mast) to colour in and to identify the three crosses there of the patron saints of England, Scotland and Ireland.

4 Ask your pupils to find out why the Saint John Ambulance Brigade uses the Maltese Cross.

5 See if your pupils can find out why people wear crosses. Is it simply for decoration; is it superstition; or does it have some religious meaning? You may be able to find a card in a Christian bookshop with this poem on it, which will help children to understand some of the religious feelings involved, particularly of wearing or having a cross out of sight:

Hot Cross Bun

Hot cross buns

It is traditional to eat Hot Cross Buns on Good Friday, although they are available in the shops these days long before Easter. The cross on them is a reminder of Jesus' death, and the spices in them remind Christians that the women went to the tomb on the Sunday morning to anoint the body of Jesus with spices, when they found the tomb empty.

Activities

It is hardly worth trying to preserve (eg. by coating in clear varnish) a hot cross bun for your artefact collection, when they are so readily available in the shops, and when it is good for children to taste them as well as learning about their significance. They can be made by following a recipe for currant buns, making sure it includes mixed spices, and by laying a pastry cross on the top before baking. As their name suggests, they are best eaten hot, and buttered.

The Cross in my Pocket

I carry a cross in my pocket;
a simple reminder to me
of the fact that I am a Christian
no matter where I may be.
This little cross is not magic,
nor is it a good luck charm.
It isn't meant to protect me
from every physical harm
It's not for identification
for all the world to see.
It's simply an understanding
between my Saviour and me.
When I put my hand in my pocket
to bring out a coin or a key,
the cross is there to remind me
of the price he paid for me.
It reminds me too to be thankful
for my blessings day by day,
and to strive to serve him better
in all that I do and say.
It's also a daily reminder
of the peace and comfort I share
with all who know my Master
and give themselves to his care.
So I carry a cross in my pocket
reminding no one but me
that Jesus Christ is Lord of my life,
if only I'll let him be.

(Copyright: Palm Tree Press)

Easter Egg

It is a Christian tradition to give eggs, mainly chocolate ones, as presents on Easter Sunday. The egg, from which comes new life, is an appropriate symbol for the day which celebrates Jesus' resurrection from the dead. The breaking of the egg can also represent the opening of the tomb in which Jesus' corpse had been buried and which was found to be empty by the disciples on Sunday morning. This is the meaning in the Orthodox Church where it is the custom, after a midnight service, to crack the hard-boiled eggs against each other with the greeting 'Christ is risen'. These eggs are usually painted red for the blood of Christ.

Activities

1 Your pupils could decorate egg-shells, preferably painting them with Christian symbols of Easter. The yolks and whites will need to have been gently blown out of their shells by putting a pin-prick in each end - a delicate operation which is not suitable for young children! (The egg can still be used for cooking).

NB If you decide it is easier for the children to use hard-boiled eggs, make sure they use non-poisonous food dyes and that the eggs are consumed as soon as possible. Do not try to keep these eggs, however beautiful the decorations, as they will go off.

Paschal Candle

The Paschal (or Easter) Candle is a large candle used in Catholic and Anglican Churches. It is usually decorated with Christian symbols such as the alpha-omega or khi-rho (see p.19), the cross and the date of the year. The priest may insert five grains of incense into the candle to represent the five wounds of Jesus.

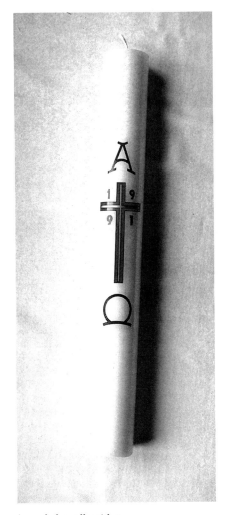

A paschal candle with a transfer on it

It is lit late on Holy Saturday in anticipation of the resurrection of Jesus Christ on Easter Sunday. Traditionally it was lit from a newly kindled fire outside the church, since the dead body of Jesus was given new life. (Two pieces of flint stone could represent this in your artefact collection.) As he lights the candle, the priest says: 'May the light of Christ, rising in glory, take away the darkness of our hearts and minds.' The candle is brought into the darkened church and the congregation's small candles are lit from it. The meaning of the Paschal Candle is summed up in the proclamation 'Christ our Light' and the ceremony represents the light of the Gospel spreading throughout the world (just as in John 8:12 Jesus says 'I am the light of the world'). Light is a symbol which is often found in Christian worship, festivals and celebrations.

After the Easter season the candle is usually placed by the font and used in baptisms.

Activities

1 Ask your pupils to think of situations in which they experience or use light. Then make a list together of all the feelings that light evokes (eg. torch-light might make them feel safe; a log fire might make them feel cosy; fireworks might make them feel excited). Discuss why Jesus is called the Light of the world.

2 Explore with pupils the meaning of 'the darkness of our hearts and minds'.

Easter cards

A selection of Easter cards.

The custom of sending greetings cards at Easter is nowhere near as popular as with Christmas cards. Those that are produced are therefore very religious, or for children, rather than catering for a wider secular market.

Activities

1 Get a selection of Easter cards for your pupils to study. Make sure they can recognise the pictures and understand their association with Easter. See if the messages inside can help them to understand the importance of Easter for Christians.

2 Your pupils could make their own Easter cards, with appropriate pictures and messages.

Baptism

Baptism involves being 'dipped' in water, and in many Christian Churches it takes place soon after a baby is born. It marks the entry of the child into the Christian family and symbolises the washing away of sin (in the case of a baby, this would mean cleansing from 'original sin'). The ceremony is popularly known as Christening, which means 'becoming Christian'. The sign of the Cross is made by the priest on the child's forehead to show that the child now belongs to Jesus. (In some Protestant Churches, such as Baptist, infants are dedicated, and Believer's Baptism takes place only when they feel ready to make a commitment to Jesus for themselves.)

Infant Baptism normally takes place inside a church building, in a special basin called a font. The font used to be placed by the main door of the church to reinforce the idea that people enter the Church through baptism. Now it is more common to have the font at the front of the church so that everybody can see the ceremony and to show that baptised Christians are full members of the Church. (Believer's Baptism is by total immersion, and therefore a special pool or baptistery is used.)

As well as the symbols of water and light, some Churches also use oil. The oil of baptism is olive oil which is rubbed onto a baby's chest to symbolise the new inner strength that baptism is believed to give to the child. The oil of chrism is a mixture of olive oil and balsam which is anointed onto the crown of the head. This represents the sealing of the gifts of the Holy Spirit. In Roman Catholic and some Anglican churches the oil of chrism is used again at confirmation. In Orthodox Churches, however, confirmation in the Holy Spirit is administered at the time of Infant Baptism.

Activities

1 In Primary Schools baptism may be looked at in a general topic on water, where different uses for water are explained. Pupils could be encouraged to think about its cleansing properties and begin to discuss statements like "I feel dirty inside", "I feel clean and new."

2 Comparisons could be made with other forms of ritual washing such as bathing in the Ganges and Islamic wudu.

3 Secondary school pupils may be able to explore St.Paul's description of baptism in Romans 6:1-4.

4 You may be able to borrow white baptismal robes from the local Baptist Church. These are used for Believer's Baptism and are weighted at the bottom so that they do not rise up in the water. This artefact can be particularly intriguing if presented as a mystery object in a problem solving activity.

Scallop shell

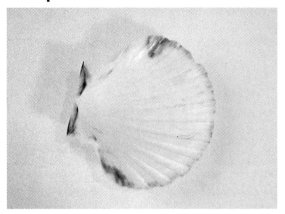

A natural scallop shell

A scallop shell, which can be natural or made of ornate metal, is used to scoop water onto the child's head, which is done three times: in the name of the Father, Son and Holy Spirit. The scallop shell is used in baptism because early Christian baptism took place by the side of a river or on a seashore. It has also become a Christian symbol for pilgrimage and shows that the newly baptised person has set out on the pilgrimage of his or her Christian life.

White garment

A white christening gown

White is a sign of innocence and of the new life of the resurrection. It is traditional for the baby to wear white at baptism.

Activities

Pupils could explore the many symbols associated with baptism ceremonies, and develop their knowledge and understanding of the underlying beliefs that Christians have about Jesus.

Baptismal candle

Baptismal candles may be simple little white candles, or candles with transfers on them, and often come in special boxes. At baptisms, the smaller candle is lit from the Paschal Candle (see p.65) and presented to the Godparents to hold for the newly baptised child. It is given with such words as 'This is to show that you have passed from darkness to light' or 'May you shine as a light in the world.' It shows that the child, like Jesus, has (symbolically) passed from death to life.

Activities

1 Children are fascinated by lighted candles. If possible, darken the room and allow pupils to observe a naked flame in silence or with appropriate music. Pupils could be given opportunities to respond creatively to this experience using art, craft, music, dance, movement or creative writing. You may wish to feed in such questions as:

What does it mean to 'shine as a light in the world'?

Can you think of anyone who has brought light into your life?

2 Some baptismal candles, particularly those in special boxes, have sufficient clues on them to be given to pupils as a useful summing-up exercise on Infant Baptism. (The example in the presentation box in the photograph touches on many aspects of baptism: the box is blue like water and has a wavy design on it; it proclaims 'Shine as a light in the world' and refers to passing from darkness into light.)

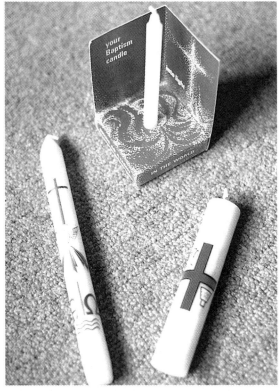

Two baptismal candles, 15cm and 23cm in length, and a small baptism candle in a special presentation box,.

Baptism certificates and cards

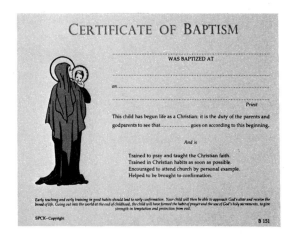

A certificate of baptism.

It is customary to send greetings cards and to give presents for a baby's baptism. The church will provide a certificate of the event.

Activities

1 Ask your pupils to consider carefully the purpose of baptism and then to choose an appropriate present for such an occasion.

2 Show your pupils a range of baptism cards and ask them to rank them according to which they think are most appropriate. They should be able to give reasons for their choices.

Holy Water containers

Holy water is water which has been blessed by a priest, like the water used in baptism; or which has come from a special holy river or spring. Pilgrims to the Holy Land often bring back water

from the River Jordan to be used for baptism, because this is the river in which Jesus himself was baptised. Lourdes in France has a special spring in which pilgrims bathe for healing; and they bring back water from there to anoint people at home. This practice is found mainly in the Catholic Church.

A small plastic water bottle in the shape of the Virgin Mary, to bring back holy water from Lourdes

Activities

1 Read the story of Jesus' baptism with your pupils (Matthew 3:13-17; Luke 3:21-22) and explore its meaning. Notice particularly the symbol of the dove, which often appears on baptismal candles and cards.

2 Your pupils may be able to find out how the spring at Lourdes was discovered by Saint Bernadette, and how this became famous as a place of healing.

3 Discuss with older pupils the dangers of superstition with many of these outward rituals of the Church (A danger which has led some Churches e.g. the Society of Friends to reject all such rituals).

Water Stoup

As you go into a Catholic Church, and in some Catholic homes, there will be a Water Stoup attached to the wall or pillar. This is to hold holy water and is a reminder to Christians of the promises made at their baptism, that they would follow Jesus. People dip their fingers in it and make the sign of the cross on themselves in the name of the Father, Son and Holy Spirit.

Two small Water Stoups produced for Roman Catholics to use at home.

Holy Communion

Holy Communion may also be called by other names, such as the Eucharist, the Mass and the Lord's Supper. It is the most important service in the Church and is done to keep Jesus' command to his disciples at the Last Supper, that they should eat bread and drink wine in remembrance of him. (Only the Salvation Army and the Society of Friends do not have such a service.)

Chalice, Paten and bread

The paten is the plate on which the Communion bread is placed before being given to the communicants, and is often made of precious metal. Some churches use ordinary bread, but it is traditional to use special round wafers which may have a cross or crucifix imprinted on them. This bread is consecrated as 'the Body of Christ'.

The chalice is the cup in which the wine is consecrated as 'the Blood of Christ'. It is often a large ornate goblet made of precious metal, but it could be a more simple version.

A pottery chalice and some Communion wafers.

Prosphora seal   (see page 18f)

Communion tots

In some Protestant Churches, the Communion wine is distributed in individual glasses, rather than everyone sharing from the same chalice. This is done for practical reasons, and people usually wait until everyone has been served so that they can all drink together.

Some small plastic Communion glasses.

Sick Call Communion set

A Sick Call Communion set

Many Churches retain some of the consecrated bread and wine from the Communion Service to be taken to those who are too ill to attend church. Little Communion sets are produced for the priest to carry this in. For practical reasons, the Roman Catholic Church usually gives only the bread to communicants, so only the wafers need be carried to sick people, and these are kept in a small container called a pyx.

First Communion Gift Set

A Roman Catholic First Communion Gift Set, containing a child's service book for the Mass, a set of Rosary Beads and a small medallion of Jesus.

First Communion Veil

In all but the Orthodox Churches, Holy Communion is withheld from very young children and there is special instruction before someone is allowed to take it. In the Anglican Church, young people or adults are usually 'confirmed' by a bishop before being allowed to take Communion; but it is the tradition in the Roman Catholic Church for children to receive their first Communion at about the age of seven, well before Confirmation. This is a big day for these children and they are dressed up for the occasion: the girls as brides of Christ, with special white veils over their heads and white dresses. They are given a certificate by the Church and cards and presents by well-wishers.

A Roman Catholic white Communion Veil.

Wedding

Many people today get married in a register office; but Christians usually still get married with a church service. They believe it is important to be married in the eyes of God ('Those whom God has joined together ...'), and to have God's blessing on their marriage and the prayers of the church.

Wedding cards

The bride and groom receive many cards to wish them happiness in their new life together. Many of these have symbols on them of a traditional church wedding.

Activities

Buy a selection of wedding cards (and wedding anniversary cards) for your artefact collection which have Christian symbols on them eg.church scenes, wedding bells, Bibles and prayer-books. Those on sale in church book shops may also have religious messages in them. Use these to help your pupils see some of the differences between a church and a registry wedding. With older pupils, study the wording of the two types of wedding service.

Wedding Garland

In the Greek Orthodox Church, bride and groom are crowned with garlands, expressing the importance and dignity of marriage.

Funeral

Funeral Service

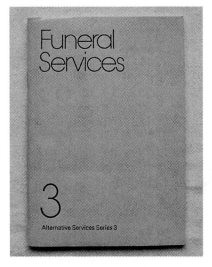

A Funeral Service booklet of the Anglican Church.

The wording of funeral services can be found in Church Prayer Books, and these will help older pupils understand some of the Christian beliefs surrounding death.

Orthodox Burial Shroud

This long piece of cloth with iconographic pictures printed on it is placed over the body in an open coffin while the funeral service takes place. Afterwards it remains over the body while the lid of the coffin is screwed down. One picture is the skull and crossbones and the

Crucifixion (in black). Above this is the Resurrection (in red) with the words 'Christ has risen'. The Christian believer is identified with Christ in his death and resurrection, and the open coffin is like a doorway to a new life.

A burial shroud

Activities

Allow the pupils to explore the imagery and symbols on the shroud. Perhaps somebody will be able to read the Greek writing on the cloth. Ask the pupils to explain what the shroud tells us about Christian belief about death and beyond.

Prayer

Christians pray privately and gathered together in small prayer-groups and at church services. The main weekly services are held on Sundays, the Christian holy day.

Prayer Books

Some Churches have a tradition of extempore prayer, which means that they make up their prayers as they go along. The only prayer which is recited from memory is the Lord's Prayer which the Lord Jesus taught to his disciples (see p76). Other Churches have set services, with some prayers repeated each time. These Churches have Prayer Books which worshippers use to follow and join in with the service.

The main Prayer Book of the Eastern Orthodox Church is the Divine Liturgy of St.John Chrysostom. The main Roman Catholic Prayer Book is The Sunday Missal; and the main one in use in the Anglican Church is the Alternative Service Book.

There are also many collections of prayers; and books of prayers and service-books specially produced for children.

Rosary Beads

Some Roman Catholics use strings of prayer-beads which are popularly called Rosaries, although strictly speaking the Rosary is the cycle of prayers which are said around the beads. The saying of the Rosary is an old tradition in the Catholic church, and while some young Catholics today have never been taught it, there is a movement in some quarters of the Catholic Church to revive the practice. The beads are passed through the thumb and forefinger of both hands, and are an aid to concentration, a means of counting off prayers and an encouragement to complete one's prayers. The prayers which are repeated are the main Christian prayers: the Our Father or Lord's Prayer, the Hail Mary and the Glory be or Gloria (see below). The creed is also recited, which sums up the main Christian beliefs; and each circuit of the beads reminds Christians of the great 'mysteries' or wonderful events associated with Jesus and Mary.

The Five Joyful Mysteries

The happy events connected with Jesus' early life:

(1) The Annunciation of the Angel Gabriel to Mary

(2) The Visitation of Mary to Elizabeth

(3) The Nativity of Jesus

(4) The Presentation of the baby Jesus in the Temple

(5) The Finding of the boy Jesus in the Temple.

The Five Sorrowful Mysteries

The sad events at the end of Jesus' life:

(1) The Agony in Gethsemane where Jesus was arrested

(2) The Scourging when Jesus was flogged by the Roman soldiers

(3) The Crowning with Thorns when Jesus was mocked by the Romans

(4) The Carrying of the Cross to his crucifixion

(5) The Death of Jesus at Calvary

The Five Glorious Mysteries

The wonderful things which are believed to have happened to Jesus Christ or Mary subsequently:

(1) The Resurrection of Jesus from the dead

(2) The Ascension of Jesus into heaven

(3) The Descent of the Holy Spirit at Pentecost

(4) The Assumption of 'Our Lady' into heaven

(5) The Coronation of 'Our Lady' as Queen of Heaven

This diagram shows how the creed and prayers are recited on particular beads, and when the Mysteries are remembered. The full Rosary entails praying round the beads three times and meditating on all fifteen Mysteries. Usually only a third (called a chaplet) is said at one time

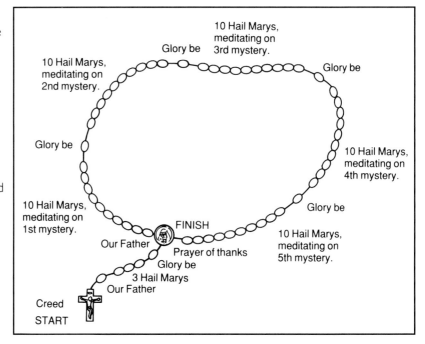

The 'Our Father'

Our Father who art in
heaven;
Hallowed be thy Name;
Thy kingdom come.

Thy will be done,
on earth as it is in heaven.
Give us this day our daily bread;
And forgive us our trespasses,
as we forgive those who trespass
against us;
And lead us not into temptation,
but deliver us from evil.
For thine is the kingdom,
the power and the glory,
for ever and ever. Amen.

The 'Hail Mary'

Hail Mary, full of grace,
the Lord is with thee.
Blessed art thou among women,
and blessed is the fruit of thy womb, Jesus.
Holy Mary, Mother of God,
pray for us sinners now
and at the hour of our death. Amen.

The 'Glory be'

Glory be the Father,
and to the Son,
and to the Holy Spirit,
As it was in the beginning,
is now and ever shall be,
world without end. Amen.

Activities

1 Your pupils could make some rosaries, being careful to put the right number of beads on the string, in the right order. They should be given a diagram of how the rosary is prayed so that they know why it is important to have the correct beads.

2 You could use some of the Mysteries to study events in the life of Jesus,

3 You could use the Glorious Mysteries, the Creed and the three prayers to study beliefs which are central to Christianity or especially associated with Roman Catholicism.

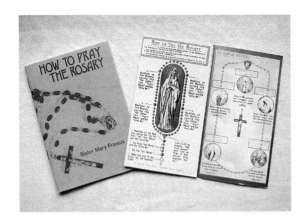

Booklets to help Catholics to use the Rosary.

Prayer Rope

This is a looped, black woollen string of knots with a tassle on the end in the shape of a Greek cross. Prayer ropes are used by many Orthodox as an aid to prayer, particularly when repeating the Jesus Prayer: 'Lord Jesus Christ, Son of the living God, have mercy upon me, sinner that I am.'

There is no set method of use. Like all prayer-beads, they help concentration by occupying the hands.

A Prayer Rope of the Orthodox Church.

Activities

1 Discuss with your pupils situations in which they find it difficult to concentrate and ways in which they might improve their concentration.

2 Your pupils could make prayer-ropes like that in the picture and use them to see if they help them to concentrate on something you read them.

Hassock

A hassock is a thick cushion for people to kneel on when they pray. They may be plain, but many are beautifully embroidered with patterns or Christian symbols.

A plain plastic hassock, or kneeler: and a tapestry one with a church bell embroidered on it

Activities

1 Explore with your pupils the significance of kneeling for prayer (making yourself small before God etc.)

2 See how many other bodily positions for prayer your pupils can discover, and think about their meanings.

3 Visit a local church with your pupils and see how many symbols they can find on the kneelers. Then find out what they mean.

Votive candle

A votive candle is usually bought in church and offered to God along with a prayer. They may be 'night-lights' in metal cases for safety, small white candles or long thin tapers. Worshippers fix their lighted candles in the stands provided, which are often placed before statues or pictures of the saints. Votive candles have always been found in Catholic and Orthodox churches; and the practice is now being revived in some Anglican churches and cathedrals, and among small groups of Christians gathered together for prayer.

Votive candles.

Activities

Find a place where the class can sit quietly in a circle, with the room darkened and a lighted candle in the centre. Get them to sit in silence, allowing time for them to relax and to soak up the atmosphere. (If this is the first time they have done this, they may only be able to remain silent for about 30 seconds at first!) Afterwards, ask them to discuss why some people find that a lighted candle helps them to pray. This will lead on to discussing what prayer is - not just talking but also 'listening' to God.

NB This exercise might be combined with the use of incense (see below).

Incense

A box of incense produced at Prinknash Abbey.

Incense is a spice which is burned over charcoal to produce a sweet fragrance. It is used in Orthodox and Catholic Churches and in some Anglican Churches. The incense is burned in a censer (also called a thurible), a container that is often made of precious metal, which allows the smoke to escape as the priest or server swings it from a chain.

People and objects in the church are censed as a sign of honour and purification. There is also a popular interpretation that the smoke rising upwards represents prayers going up to God. Many Christians also find that the smell of incense makes the atmosphere more conducive to prayer.

Activities

Buy some joss sticks (which are easier and safer to use in school than incense and have a similar effect), and burn one for your pupils to smell while you are explaining about incense.

NB This could be combined with the activity on votive candles above, since both contribute to an atmosphere which some people find helpful for prayer.

You may be able to buy an incense holder used in Greek Orthodox homes. They are inexpensive, and can range from a clay pot to a metal container with a lid.

Icon

A postcard of an icon, mounted on a block of wood.

An icon is a special holy picture associated with the Eastern Orthodox Churches. Painting an icon is regarded as a religious task to be done prayerfully, and is often done by monks. Icons portray Jesus or the Saints, in a semi-lifelike style according to traditional rules with the full face always shown (so that the eyes seem to follow you around) even if the body is sideways. When completed, they are blessed by a priest and used in worship either in church or in the home. Eastern Orthodox churches can be recognised by the many icons which fill the walls and the icon-screen (iconostasis) across the front of the church. Worshippers pray before icons and kiss them to show their respect for the saints who are portrayed there.

Activities

1 Genuine icons are obviously expensive and, as holy objects, may not be suitable for keeping in an artefact collection. If you can find postcards of icons, these can be stuck onto pieces of chip-board of the same size to make a replica of an icon. Indeed, this sort can be bought in Christian shops. Your pupils may like to help you with this.

2 Find a picture of an icon for each pupil to have. Give them time to look at them quietly before writing down their impressions.

Statues

Some Christians do not agree with the portrayal of saints in pictures and statues because of the danger of idolatry. However, as with icons for Orthodox Christians, statues have an important place in the worship of Roman Catholics and many Anglicans. There will nearly always be a statue of the Blessed Virgin Mary with the young Jesus in a Catholic church, and other saints as well. Some Catholics have small statues in their homes.

Activities

1 Explain to your pupils what idolatry means. See if they can understand the difference between an image which helps someone to worship God and an idol which is worshipped instead of God.

2 If you are studying Roman Catholicism with older pupils, ask a Catholic to speak to your class about the importance of Mary (whom they call 'Our Lady') in the Catholic tradition.

A wooden statue (20 cm high) of Mary with Jesus

A painted statue of Saint Patrick, popular with Irish Catholics.

money is brought up to the front of the church and dedicated to God's service. Many Christians take out a covenant which commits them to give a certain amount of their earnings (and allows the church, as a charity, to reclaim the tax paid on that money).

Missionary Collection Box

A collection box for the United Society for the Propogation of the Gospel

It is a tradition for Christian supporters of Missionary Societies to have their own collection boxes at home, which are emptied by the society once a year.

Sometimes, churches have special appeals at particular times of year, like Lent, when individual collection boxes are provided to raise money for some project in the Church.

Offerings

From the days of the Early Church, Christians helped the needy among them and gave financial support to the work of the Church. This still continues today. Offerings are made during church services where the

Activities

1 See if any local churches or missionary societies will provide you with collection boxes for your artefact collection. Use them to discuss with older pupils the Christian idea of 'stewardship' of our resources.

2 Ask your pupils to try to find out what happens to the money which is put into the church collection plate at their local church.

3 Ask a few pupils to write to Christian Third World agencies e.g. Christian Aid, Tear Fund and CAFOD, to find out how they use the money which is donated to them.

Vestments

Church vestments are the traditional robes worn by those leading the service, and are worn in the Orthodox, Catholic and Anglican Churches. The ministers of other Churches wear very basic robes or everyday clothes.

Liturgical colours

The following colours are used for vestments and church hangings at particular times during the church's calendar.

PURPLE for the times of preparation at Advent, Lent

WHITE for the times of celebration at Christmas, Epiphany, Easter, Ascension

RED for the fire of the Holy Spirit at Whitsun and for the blood of the martyrs on Saints' Days

GREEN for the growth of the church during Pentecost (formerly called Trinity)

Stole

A hand-made stole 200cm length.

A stole is a long thin strip of material which clergy hang round their necks as a sign of office. Its origin is uncertain: suggestions range from the Roman pallium which was a sign of status, to a servant's towel as a sign of humble service. It can be plain or very ornate, and usually matches the set of vestments, which come in different liturgical colours (see opposite).

Activities

1 See if two of your pupils would help make two simple stoles for your artefact collection and for display. One should be made from a strip of red material on one side and white on the other. The other should be made from a strip of green material on one side and purple on the other. Before sewing them together, a Christian symbol could be embroidered at each end on both sides. Make sure all your pupils know why these four colours were used.

2 Ask a local priest to show your pupils the church vestments and to explain when and how they are worn and their significance. This will be particularly fascinating if you have an Orthodox Church within reach.

3 Set your pupils the task of designing a modern set of church vestments for a particular Christian festival.

The Salvation Army

The Salvation Army is well-known for its social work, but many people do not realise that it is a Christian denomination (a Church) in its own right. It has its own distinctive organisation, creed, worship and places of worship. Founded in Victorian London, it also has a practical concern for inner city deprivation.

Flag

The Salvation Army flag is in its three symbolic colours with an emblem in the centre. The outer border of dark blue stands for the purity of God the Father. The inner rectangle of dark red stands for the blood of Christ, and the yellow star in the centre stands for the fire of the Holy Spirit, (as do the words 'Blood and Fire'). A large flag is carried when the Salvation Army bands go out onto the streets.

Salvation Army Tricolour flag, medium size 40 cm by 49 cm.

Activities

1 Work could be done on symbolic colours eg. ask your pupils what colours we associate with the different seasons of the year or with different emotions. (What colour is Summer? What colour is sadness?)

2 The Trinity is symbolised by the three colours: blue, red and yellow. Ask your pupils if these are the colours they would choose for God the Father, God the Son and God the Holy Spirit. Or simply ask them what colour they would choose to represent God, and to explain why.

Doll in Salvation Army uniform

The uniform of the Salvation Army is easily recognised by the public. It also shows the military aspect of this Church which believes in discipline and ranks its members from Junior Soldiers through to the General at its head. The basic uniform is made from navy serge with red trimmings. The letter 'S' for 'Salvation' always appears on the collars as well as a badge to indicate rank. Men have caps and women bonnets, which they wear with such pride that it is unlikely you would get one for your artefact collection. This doll, however, and other models of Salvation Army figures are available from the Salvationist Souvenirs Catalogue (see p12).

Activities

Ask your pupils to discuss the advantages and the disadvantages of Church people being easily recognised by what they wear.

A doll, 20 cm high, dressed in the traditional Salvation Army navy uniform.

Islamic artefacts

Contents

Scriptures

Muslims have only one holy book, the Arabic Qur'an, which they believe to contain the words of God; but they also study the Hadith for guidance, which contain Muhammad's teachings.

Qur'an

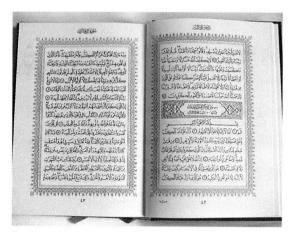

Copies of the Qur'an in Arabic

The Qur'an is the holy book of Islam. Muslims believe it is the perfect and final revelation of God (Allah) to humanity. They believe that it was revealed to their Prophet Muhammad through the Angel Gabriel, who learnt the words and recited them to the people. Soon after Muhammad's death they were collected and written down in a book. The word qur'an means 'recitation', and passages from the Qur'an are still recited by Muslims today.

The Qur'an is in Arabic, the language in which it was first given (Muhammad lived in Arabia). Arabic is written from right to left, and therefore an Arabic Qur'an opens in this direction (the opposite to an English book). Pages may be decorated with a patterned border.

Muslims take particular care of their Qur'ans because this book is so important to them. They believe that it contains the very words of God in which he teaches them what they should believe and how they should live. When not in use, they keep their copies wrapped up, on a high shelf with nothing on top of them. If they want to carry one around with them, they can get small copies with covers which zip up for protection.

Activities

1 Send your pupils to wash their hands before allowing them to touch a copy of the Qur'an. Explain that many Muslims, before reading the Qur'an, would go through the same ritual as they do before prayer (i.e. washing their hands, arms, face, head and feet, removing their shoes, and covering their heads if they are women). Ask them what this treatment of the book shows about the Muslim attitude to the Qur'an. Encourage them to discuss how far we should show respect to other people's precious belongings by treating them in the same way as they do.

2 Ask your pupils to decide the most appropriate place to keep a copy of the Qur'an in the classroom, and to discuss the practical and symbolic reasons for keeping the Qur'an in a high place.

3 Ask your pupils, in small groups, to find out all they can about the Qur'an by closely investigating a copy.

4 Give your pupils a few words of Arabic to copy, insisting that they write from right to left. You might use this common Muslim greeting: Assalamu alaikum meaning 'Peace be with you.'

5 Muslims who do not live in Arabic-speaking countries still have to learn to read the Qur'an in Arabic. See if your pupils can find out where and how they would do this. (Various videos on Islam show scenes from mosque schools which children attend after day school or at weekends.)

6 If you have a school copy of the Qur'an, make sure it has a nice clean cover. A square of material the size of a headscarf could be wrapped round it; a pupil may like to sew it into an envelope shape, as shown in the diagram.

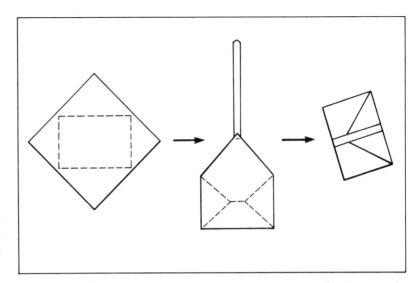

Qur'an stand

Traditional folding book-stands, used for the Qur'an.

It is customary in Muslim countries to sit on the floor. These ornately hand carved wooden book stands are a useful way of raising the Qur'an off the floor when reading it, and so keeping it clean. Muslims sit cross-legged behind them.

Activities

1 Some of your pupils may like to make Qur'an stands for your artefact collection. They can be made from thin plywood (with a little help from the Technology department!) or thick cardboard. Pupils will need to look carefully at the shape and folding-action of an example. The patterned effect can be achieved by drawing it on paper and sticking this over the basic wooden or cardboard shape.

2 Allow pupils to sit on the floor, cross-legged, with the book stand, and discuss why it is important for Muslims to keep the Qur'an off the floor.

Interpretations of the Qur'an

Muslims believe that every word of the Qur'an, every letter, comes from God. Therefore the true Qur'an is the Arabic Qur'an, the language in which it was originally revealed. It may be helpful to have it translated into different languages (and Muslims sometimes use copies which have the Arabic on one page and their spoken language on the opposite page), but these are not accepted as genuine Qur'ans. They are treated as interpretations of the Qur'an, because changes of meaning are inevitable when something is put into another language.

Two well-established English interpretations of the Qur'an, by Arberry and Pickthall.

Activities

1 Consider with your pupils the difficulties of translating something into another language. See if they can think of English idioms, for instance, which do not exist in other languages (e.g. to be 'fed up').

2 Ask your pupils to list, in two columns, the advantages and disadvantages of keeping religious scriptures in their original languages.

3 See if your pupils can find out which other religions keep their holy books in their original languages.

Hadith

The Hadith are authenticated 'reports' of what the Prophet Muhammad said or did. Unlike the Qur'an, they are not claimed to be the words of God, but are Muhammad's own words or actions. Since Muslims try to follow Muhammad's example, they are second in authority to the Qur'an for teaching them how to live.

There are six main collections of Hadith which run into many volumes and are expensive and not suitable for schools; but it is possible to find small selections of Hadith which secondary school pupils may find interesting.

Some pages of a book called 'Selection from Hadith' in both Arabic and English.

Activities

1 Ask your pupils to find out from the Hadith what Muslims write (and say) whenever they mention Muhammad. (It is sometimes abbreviated in writing to 'Pbuh' i.e. 'Peace be upon him'.)

2 Ask your pupils to look through a selection of Hadith in order to make a list of some of the names which are written under them. These are the names of the Muslims who made collections of the Hadith. The two most authoritative are given the title Sahih meaning 'trustworthy' (i.e. Sahih Muslim and Sahih Al-Bukhari).

3 If you have older pupils who are studying a particular aspect of Islam (like Pilgrimage), find some Hadith on it and ask them to write down what these passages teach Muslims on this matter.

Prayer

Muslims are required to perform ritual prayers (salah) five times a day, so that they remember God repeatedly from early in the morning to last thing at night. They must prepare themselves properly for prayer by washing their hands, arms, face, head and feet, and must dress decently. Salah consists of going through set prayer movements while praising God and reciting short passages from the Qur'an.

Prayer mat

A prayer-mat, 0.5 metre by 1 metre in size.

A prayer-mat with a compass affixed, showing the instruction booklet attached to the back.

Muslims must have a clean place for prayer because they prostrate themselves before God by kneeling on the ground with their foreheads touching the ground. They remove their shoes, wash their feet and may stand on a prayer-carpet, or prayer-mat. Each prayer-mat should have an arch design on it, so that it is laid down in the correct direction for prayer, pointing towards the Ka'ba in Makkah (Mecca). They are usually decorated with Islamic patterns and may show the Ka'ba and the Prophet Muhammad's mosque in Madinah or some other mosque.

Activities

1 Your pupils could make some prayer-mats with large sheets of plain paper or by weaving together wide strips of coloured sugar-paper (green, blue and yellow are traditional Muslim colours). A paper fringe can be made and stuck to the top and bottom of the mat. The border can be decorated with a geometric pattern and the outline of an arch drawn in the centre section.

2 Ask your pupils to try to find out why patterns are so important in Islamic art, and why they will not see pictures of people or animals on Muslim prayer-mats.

3 Discuss with your pupils the significance of bodily prostration in prayer. Then make a list together of other positions people take up for prayer (limiting this to Islam if you wish). Divide the class into small groups and give each group the description of one prayer-position. Ask them to write down any practical purposes in the position they have been asked to consider and also whether it has any symbolic significance.

Compass

Muslims all over the world use a special compass to find the direction of Makkah in Saudi Arabia. They need to know this 'direction' (the quiblah), because they all pray facing the Ka'ba, the central shrine of Islam which is in the Sacred Mosque at Makkah.

The compass comes with an instruction booklet on how to find the qiblah from the main cities in the world. These compasses usually have a picture of the Ka'ba in the centre and a picture of a minaret on the outer circle which will point in the direction of the Ka'ba when the compass is set properly. (A minaret is the tower of the mosque from which people are called to prayer.)

Activities

1 Ask your pupils to use a Muslim compass to find the qiblah from your school's location.

2 Ask your pupils to draw a diagram with the Ka'ba in the centre and arrows showing the direction of prayer from all round the world. This should help them to discuss the significance of having one central focal point in Islam (e.g. unity, brotherhood).

3 See if your pupils can find out why the Ka'ba has become the centre of Islam.

For further information and activities on the Islamic compass, see pages 21 to 23.

Head coverings

A man's prayer cap and traditional Arab head-dress.

A white crocheted or embroidered cap, or some other hat, is often worn by Muslim men when they pray. It is not obligatory, but it holds their hair in place when they go through the prayer movements, particularly when bowing and prostrating themselves on the ground.

The traditional Arab head-dress for men is a large scarf, used to protect their heads and necks from the desert sun. It would be perfectly acceptable for Arab Muslims to wear this in prayer.

Women cover their heads with large scarves when they pray because this is considered modest. The scarves provided at mosques for visitors are often of a fine white material, but they could be any colour and patterned.

Activities

1 Ask your pupils why Islamic prayer hats cannot have peaks or brims. (They should think of the prayer-movements.)

2 You may be able to get hold of a genuine Arab head-dress (since they are on sale to tourists in Arab countries). If not, you could improvise with a square of thin cotton cloth (100 cm square) and some rope to tie round it. It should be worn as shown in the diagram.

3 See if your pupils know of other customs of covering or uncovering the head in special places (eg. men remove their hats in church) or to show respect in the presence of other people.

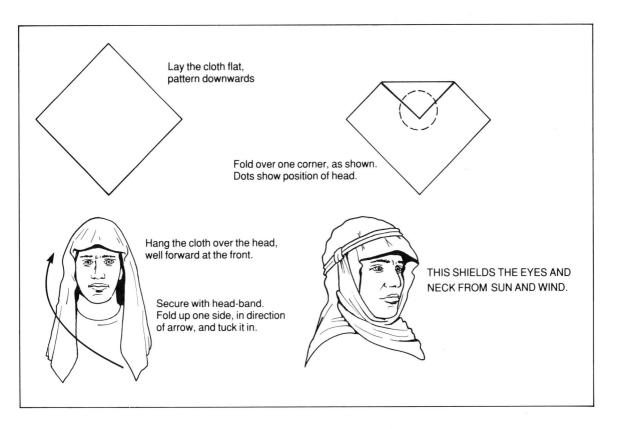

Lay the cloth flat, pattern downwards

Fold over one corner, as shown. Dots show position of head.

Hang the cloth over the head, well forward at the front.

Secure with head-band. Fold up one side, in direction of arrow, and tuck it in.

THIS SHIELDS THE EYES AND NECK FROM SUN AND WIND.

Prayer-beads

Two strings of prayer-beads, one with 99 beads, the other with 33.

Islamic prayer-beads are called subha (and also by the rarer term, misbahah). Some Muslims refer to the beads as tasbih, but this really describes the action of using the beads.

The beads are threaded loosely on a string, with the knotted end usually finished off with a tassle. Each string has either 99 beads or 33. Those with 99 are divided into sets of 33 by 3 'rogue' beads.

The telling of prayer-beads (as the action is called) is done by passing each bead through the thumb and forefinger. It is done to keep count of prayers like 'Glory be to God', 'All praise be to God' and 'God is the greatest' (each of which is said 33 times); or to keep count of the 99 'Beautiful Names' or attributes of God in the Qur'an. Not all Muslims use them.

Activities

1 Your pupils could make subhas for your artefact collection. They could use any type or colour of beads, and should follow the details in the description above. Discuss with them the importance of having the correct number of beads (because of the Beautiful Names).

2 Give your pupils a copy of the first chapter of the Qur'an and ask them to find some of the Names or descriptions used there for God.

Festivals

The two main festivals of Islam are Eid ul Fitr which comes at the end of Ramadan, the month of fasting; and Eid ul Adha which comes at the end of Hajj, the Great Pilgrimage. As with festivals in other religions, there are special religious services, and celebrations with cards, presents, parties, new clothes and good food. They also remember the poor and needy at these times.

Eid cards

A variety of Eid cards.

Muslims send each other greetings cards at festival times. The cards wish people Eid Mubarak - 'Happy Festival'. They may be decorated with intricate Muslim patterns, or show Muslim centres. Since they have Arabic writing in them, they should open from right to left, but some of those on sale in England open in the same way as English cards.

Activities

1 Collect as many Eid cards as possible, and see what your pupils can learn from them about Islam.

2 Set your pupils the task of making their own Eid cards. They need to consider the rules of Islamic art (eg. no realistic figurative art of natural things) and the way that the card should open. They should use the traditional Muslim greeting given above.

Mendhi

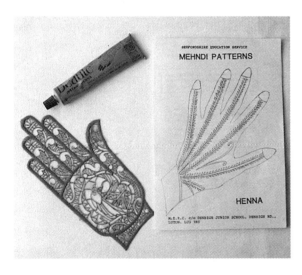

A tube of Mendhi paste (henna) and a stencil for a hand-design.

The Indian custom of women painting the palms of their hands for festivals is found among Muslims from India and Pakistan, as well as Hindus. Henna dye, which stains the skin orange, is applied with the end of a match-stick to make beautiful patterns.

Activities

1 If you are studying the ways in which Muslims celebrate their festivals, your pupils may enjoy decorating their own hands with washable ink (since henna stains for several days), or drawing around their hands on a piece of paper and decorating the shapes for display.

(See also page 109, for the Hindu use of Mehndi.)

Teachings

Islamic books

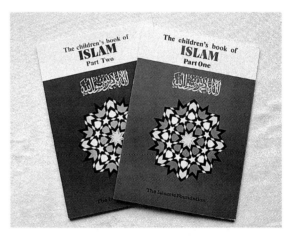

A selection of Islamic books to teach Muslim children their religion.

It is useful to have among your Islamic artefacts a selection of Islamic books which Muslims themselves use to learn about their religion. These can be obtained from mosques or Islamic bookshops and include children's story books and colouring books. You might also find little handbooks for Muslims going on Pilgrimage.

Islamic posters and postcards

A set of postcards showing the places visited on Hajj, the Great Pilgrimage in Makkah.

There are posters available showing different aspects of Islam, like the Five Pillars; or photographs of famous Islamic places like the Prophet's Mosque in Madinah. Postcards are also interesting, and easier to keep in good condition in your artefact collection.

Older pupils may like to consider why there are so few artefacts or sacred objects used in Islam. It is to do with the prohibition of images? Are objects an obstacle to the believer's direct relationship with Allah?

Islamic decorations

A shiny Islamic car sticker with the Bismillah in Arabic calligraphy.

You may come across examples of calligraphy on framed wall-decorations or painted plates as well as inexpensive car-stickers These often have famous Islamic verses on them, such as the Shahada, the declaration of belief that 'There is no God but Allah, and Muhammad is the Messenger of Allah', or the Bismillah with which most chapters of the Qur'an open: 'In the name of God, the Merciful, the Compassionate.'

A decorative plate with the Shahada painted on it.

Hindu
artefacts

Contents

Introduction

Most of the artefacts described here are associated with the different Hindu deities. It is important to realise that in Hinduism, the different deities are different expressions of the One Reality which Hindus know as Brahman. A famous passage from the Rig Veda (one of the most ancient of Hindu sacred writings) illustrates this:

"They call him Indra, Mitra, Varuna, Agni or the heavenly sunbird Garutman. The seer calls in many ways that which is One." (Rig Veda 1. 164 v46)

Hindus describe this idea in different ways. For example:
the different deities are like stepping stones in order to reach union with Brahman
or
the different deities are like different facets of the one diamond. Whilst each facet of the diamond gives light of a particular colour (and there are many) the diamond itself is One.

In Hinduism there are three main deities: Brahma (not to be confused with Brahman), Vishnu and Shiva. Associated with these three are various other deities such as Ganesha, Hanuman and so on. An attempt is made here to demonstrate the relationships and characteristics of the most significant deities in Hindu worship.

It is fairly easy to purchase statues of the different Hindu gods and goddesses. The most easily available are made of plastic and are very brightly coloured. The more aesthetic statues are not so easy to find and are made of wood, brass and stone.

Posters are readily available and are included in this book because they are often used in Hindu worship. These posters are particularly good for work on the different symbols associated with each deity.

A trimurti, showing Brahma, Vishnu and Shiva in one statue.

Brahma and Sarasvati

Although Brahma was the "uncreated creator" and the source of all creation, he is by no means as popular as Vishnu and Shiva. In fact very few temples are dedicated to Brahma and in many ways his wife Sarasvati is more important in Hindu worship.

Brahma - from a Hindu comic.

From the poster of Brahma, notice the following:

The four heads. They may represent:

- the four Vedas (Sacred writings)

- the four Yugas (eras/ages of time)

- the four Varnas (castes)

The four heads may also demonstrate that Brahma sees in all directions and therefore knows everything.

The four arms represent the four quarters of the world - ie the whole of creation for which he is responsible.

Other symbols to look out for are:

The prayer beads which represent prayer and the position of the hands which suggest "Do not fear".

The spoon represents the offerings made in Hindu worship (see puja tray page 108.)

The water container shows that Brahma was the first living being and that he came from out of the ocean.

The small book represents the Vedas.

Many of the Hindu gods and godesses have vehicles or steeds which are associated with them. Brahma is often depicted riding a swan which is a symbol of wisdom. This again shows that Brahma knows everything there is to know.

Statuette of Sarasvati

Sarasvati is Brahma's wife and is the goddess of learning. Hindus will therefore pray to her when they are about to take an examination or are involved in study of any kind. In fact her name is derived from "swara" which means "sound" as during creation Sarasvati gave Brahma the sound by which he created the Vedas. She is also called Vagdevi which means goddess of speech and therefore of learning.

The statue illustrated here shows her with four arms which represent mind, intellect, conscience and ego. She is holding prayer beads and a book which represent true wisdom and learning. She is often depicted playing a musical instrument (a Veena) as she is also the goddess of music, art and literature. Her vehicle is a white goose which signifies beauty and grace. Sometimes she is also shown riding a white swan or a peacock. Sometimes we see her rising out of a pink lotus flower.

Activities

1 In order to develop the idea of symbol or representation with younger pupils, you may wish to start off with games such as:
If I were a bird, what kind of bird would I be?
If I were a colour......
If you were an animal....
and so on, so as to explore the characteristics of animals, plants etc.

2 Leading on from the first activity pupils could explore the way in which Brahma is shown as all-knowing by giving him four heads. What other ways could we represent wisdom?

3 Pupils could draw the statues of Brahma and Sarasvati. They could label the symbols and explain their significance.

4 Older pupils could do some research on the four Vedas, Yugas and Varnas.

Vishnu

Statuette of Vishnu

Vishnu is one of the most popular deities in Hinduism and regarded as "The Preserver", the one who intervenes to preserve or protect the law (dharma) in the world.

The word "Vishnu" itself means "one who pervades" as Vishnu, we shall see, comes to earth in various forms to defeat evil. He is also known as Naryana which could mean: One who is the dwelling place of all human beings, or One who is the ultimate goal of all humanity.

Often Vishnu is depicted as being dark blue in colour, which is a symbol of cosmic power. One of his most recognisable features is the mark upon his forehead. This is also worn by deities associated with him and by those who follow him (Vaishnavites). He is sometimes shown as seated on a throne, which on closer scrutiny, is the thousand headed serpent Ananta. Ananta means "infinite" and represents cosmic time which is eternal.

As with some of the other Hindu deities, Vishnu's four arms represent his power over the four corners of the world and of the cosmos. In each of his hands he holds an object which tells us something about his character.

• **the conch shell** is used as a signal in battle and here represents the five elements of earth, water, fire, wind and air.

• **the discus and the mace** are weapons and represent the cosmic mind and intellect.

• **the lotus** is a commonly used symbol in Hindu art and represents purity, the enlightened mind and the fully evolved world. The lotus flower is remarkable in the way it grows out of the muddy water and yet still remains undirtied and pure. Devotees too, by fixing their minds on Vishnu, can remain untouched by the impurities of the world and thus achieve perfection.

Other symbols associated with Vishnu are:

• **the bow** which represents the cosmic senses and

• **the sword** which signifies wisdom.

Vishnu's steed or vehicle is a large bird-like creature called Garuda which means "wings of speech". The speech refers to the Vedas. Often Garuda carries symbols similar to Vishnu and two of his hands are in the position of adoration for his Lord and Master.

Activities

1 Pupils could draw a picture of Vishnu and Garuda. They could label the various symbols and explain their significance.

2 Pupils, on noting Vishnu's blue skin, may wish to explore the symbolic use of colour. This could begin with colour used in daily life and then move on to the symbolic use of colour in different religions.

3 Older pupils may wish to deepen their understanding of the Hindu concept of Dharma.

Lakshmi

Vishnu's wife or consort is known as Lakshmi and she is the goddess of prosperity. If people are in financial difficulty, or setting out on financial ventures, they will pray to her. Farmers also pray to her in order to achieve a good harvest.

Statuette of Lakshmi

Lakshmi is especially popular at Divali. People put lamps in their windows in order to attract her attention. They hope that she will visit them and make their homes prosperous for the coming New Year.

In Hindu art Lakshmi is often seen with Airavata, the King of the elephants. This is a reference to when she came out of the ocean together with Airavata. At the time, it seems the gods and the demons were churning the ocean in an attempt to locate Amrit, a magical drink which would give them immortality.

In her hands she holds lotus flowers. The other hands are in a posture of giving, indeed one is releasing gold coins, showing that she is the goddess of prosperity and good fortune.

Lakshmi is often shown with a pink complexion which signifies her kindness to all. In fact many Hindus revere her as the Divine Mother.

Activities

1 Pupils may wish to draw a picture of Lakshmi. They could then label all the symbols and explain their significance.

2 They may be able to find out more about the incident when the gods were churning the ocean.

3 Pupils could describe how Hindus pay particular attention to Lakshmi during the festival of Divali.

The avatars of Vishnu

The Bhagavata Purana teaches that Vishnu, as the Supreme Being, came down to earth on several occasions and in different forms to destroy evil and to protect the world. These appearances of Vishnu are called avatars as avatar means "to come down".

A dashavatar, which depicts all ten avatars of Vishnu

There are ten main avatars:

1	Matsya	-	a fish
2	Kurma	-	a tortoise
3	Varaha	-	a boar
4	Narasinha	-	a man-lion
5	Vamana	-	a dwarf
6	Parasurama	-	Rama, the devotee with a battle-axe
7	Rama	-	Rama, the Prince
8	Krishna	-	the great Teacher
9	Buddha	-	the religious leader
10	Kalki	-	The Saviour who is yet to come. He is depicted as riding a white horse and brandishing a shining sword.

You may be able to purchase a dashavatar which literally means "ten avatars". It depicts all ten avatars of Vishnu, but they are not so easy to find in this country. The two main avatars are of course Rama and Krishna.

Activities

1 Pupils could find out more about the ten avatars of Vishnu. They could draw them and write brief notes about each one.

2 They may wish to do more extensive work on one or two of the avatars.

3 It may be possible to invite a Hindu into the classroom who is knowledgeable about the ten avatars. It would be particularly interesting to explore the mysterious avatar Kalki who is regarded as the future Saviour.

Rama

Prince Rama is the hero of the Ramayana which is celebrated every year during the festival of Divali.

An image reminding Hindus of the Ramayana story.

The story is so well known that only the briefest outline is given here:

The demon king Ravana causes so much havoc in the world that Vishnu intervenes by appearing again on the earth, this time in the form of Prince Rama.

For various reasons Rama is exiled in the forest, together with his wife Sita and his brother Lakshmana. Ravana with much guile succeeds in abducting Sita and imprisons her on the island of Sri Lanka. After countless adventures Rama, together with Lakshmana and Hanuman, the monkey god, destroys Ravana and rescues his beloved wife Sita.

This well-loved story contains many themes. There is of course the victory of good over evil, light over darkness, which is why it is celebrated at Divali. The symbol of light is all pervading.

There is the theme of friendship and loyalty in the face of insurmountable obstacles. This is shown by Lakshmana and especially by Hanuman, who together with all the creatures of the forest succeeds in building a vast bridge which joined mainland India with Sri Lanka.

Lastly there is the theme of fidelity in marriage. Rama is afraid that Sita, in her captivity, has been forced to submit to Ravana's desire. However, she emerges as chaste as before and Rama and Sita are regarded in Hindu culture as a model for married couples to imitate today.

Hanuman

Activities

1 Pupils can find out more information about Rama by reading a shortened edition of the Ramayana.

2 They could make masks for the main characters and re-enact the story of the Ramayana.

3 There is a BBC computer programme on the Ramayana which is designed for 5-7 year olds. It enables them to familiarise themselves with the story by building up their own picture boards.

Krishna

Vishnu came to earth in the form of Krishna to give his teachings to mankind. You can read these teachings in the Bhagavad Gita (see page 103).

The theme of devotion to Krishna is developed in a very different way through other writings known as the Puranas. Here we find mythological stories about Krishna's birth, his mischievous childhood, his ability to slay dreadful demons, and of his love affairs with the gopis (cowherdesses) and especially of his love for the gopi Radha. Krishna is easily recognised by the flute that he carries, his blue skin, the mark of Vishnu, and often he is wearing a peacock's feather.

Radha and Krishna.

This shows the love between Krishna and the gopi Radha. On one level the accounts of the courtship between Krishna and Radha seem to be merely erotic stories. However, it is important to understand their symbolic nature: Krishna represents God and Radha represents the soul of the devotee. The love and sexual union between Radha and Krishna represents the intimate rapport necessary between God and the believer.

One incident reported in the Puranas illustrates this idea:

One day Krishna came across Radha and the gopis bathing in the river. He stole their clothes and hid up a tree. Soon one of the girls realised their clothes had gone and discovered Krishna was responsible. They pleaded with him to return the clothes, but he insisted that they would only be returned if the girls came out of the river with their hands above their heads. Naturally the girls, being modest, protest but eventually have to comply with Krishna's wishes. This story has been interpreted in the following way: Krishna, as God wants the devotee to come to him completely naked, in other words hiding nothing and being completely poor before God.

Activities

1 Visit a Hindu Temple or Mandir which is dedicated to Krishna. Ask the pupils to pay particular attention to the way Krishna is portrayed and revered.

2 Pupils can read about the childhood of Krishna in the Puranas, or in Hindu comics (see page111). They could then illustrate some of these stories.

The Bhagavad Gita

The Bhagavad Gita is one of the most loved and revered of Hinduism's Sacred Writings. It is just one book, one episode, from the massive epic, the Mahabharata.

The scene is a battlefield in which two families are poised to destroy each other. The Bhagavad Gita contains the conversation between Arjuna and his charioteer Krishna. In reality the scene is a vehicle for Krishna to give his teachings on the path to salvation, which is through the way of Yoga and through the way of devotion to Krishna himself.

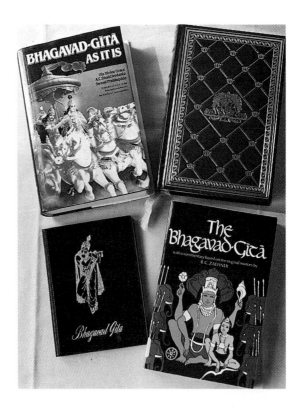

Copies of the Bhagavad Gita are easy to obtain. They can be purchased as leatherbound classics or as paperbacks in English. It is also available with a commentary such as "The Bhagavad Gita As It Is." These usually contain excellent illustrations and they contain verses from the Bhagavad Gita in Sanscrit together with an English Commentary.

Activities

1 Older pupils could read extracts from the Bhagavad Gita. They could choose passages which they find of interest and make them into an illuminated manuscript.

2 It may be possible to invite a Hindu into the classroom who can talk about what the Bhagavad Gita means to him or her.

Shiva

We have already described Shiva in his cosmic dance as Shiva Nataraja on page 24. Together, with Vishnu, he is one of the most popular deities worshipped in Hinduism.

A poster of Shiva

The Shiva linga

The word Shiva itself means "kindly" and "auspicious". He is also known as "Mahadeva" (great God) and "Mahayogi" (great Ascetic). Many of the artefacts associated with Shiva are full of sexual imagery. They are symbols of fertility and therefore geared more to older pupils. For example the Shiva Linga pictured here is basically a symbol of the male and female sexual union which in turn represents the creative energy of Shiva.

This story about Shiva Linga is more appropriate for children. One day the gods Brahma and Vishnu were quarrelling over which of them was the greatest, when a flaming column of light suddenly appeared before them. They agreed to hold a competition to see who could reach the end of the column first. Brahma took the form of his goose and flew upwards, while

Vishnu took of the form of a boar and dived downwards. But the higher Brahma flew, and the lower Vishnu dived, the further the column extended itself until it became clear that it had no end. Then a voice was heard from the centre of the pillar 'I am Shiva, the Great God. All forms are but forms of me.' So the Shiva Linga, a stone column, is a symbol of the greatness of Shiva.

Shiva is often accompanied by the white bull "Nandi". The bull is also a symbol of fertility and of animal instincts. The fact that Nandi is Shiva's companion, shows that Shiva, as Lord of the Ascetics, has mastered all the senses. Shiva is easily recognisable in Hindu art by the Trident which he carries and the three horizontal lines painted on his forehead. Devotees of Shiva (Shaivites) also paint their foreheads with the same design.

Shakti
(the power of Shiva - seen here in three forms)

Parvati

Parvati is the wife of Shiva. She represents the power (Shakti) by which Shiva creates, sustains and destroys the universe. She is the female aspect of creation (Shakti) and displays different characteristics.

Parvati (or Uma) is Shakti in her most gentle form. As the daughter of the Himalayas she is depicted with snow white skin. She has four arms: two hands hold lotus flowers and the other two are in the position of giving.

Durga

Statuette of Shiva and Parvati.

Here Shakti is seen in the form of Durga which means "one who is difficult to approach" Here she is seen riding a Tiger. Durga is ferocious, carries countless weapons and destroys Mahisasura, the demon of ignorance and selfishness. This is a powerful demon and humans need help from the Durga the "Divine Mother" in order to defeat these two evils.

Kali

Kali is Shakti in an awesome and terrifying form. She is dark in colour, with a red face and her tongue hanging out. She is depicted in a cremation ground with one foot on the body of Shiva. She wears a necklace of human skulls and carries a severed head which is dripping with blood.

This image of Kali is rich in symbolism and depicts the end of an age. Hinduism has many different ages or epochs and Kali here is seen bringing one of them to an end. The world has to be destroyed in order for it to be recreated again.

In this statue Kali's hands represent cosmic energy. The fifty skulls represent the letters of the alphabet as the letters represent sound and sound represents creation. The severed head represents cosmic upheaval and global destruction. In many ways Kali's dance of destruction echoes Shiva's cosmic dance.

Why is Kali dancing on the body of Shiva? It seems that he is using his body to absorb the terrifying impact of her dance and suddenly, realising what she has done, Kali puts out her tongue, which is a sign of embarrassment in Southern India.

Shiva here is still in total control. He is the source of all energy and Kali here personifies the effective power of Shiva. It is interesting to note however, that in many parts of India Shiva's power or Shakti, depicted in the female form, has become more important than Shiva himself, and is worshipped as the Divine Mother.

Activities

1 See the activities associated with Shiva Nataraj on page 24.

2 Ask pupils to draw pictures of the different expressions of Shakti: Parvati, Durga and Kali. They could then label the different symbols and explain their significance.

3 Older pupils may do some research on Yoga and asceticism in Hinduism.

4 If possible visit a Hindu Temple or Mandir and see the area devoted to Shiva. Ask one of the devotees to explain how they pay homage to Shiva and to his consorts.

5 Durga helps her devotees to overcome ignorance and selfishness. Why might these be regarded as evils? What other evils can pupils name?

Ganesha

Ganesha (or Ganesh in Southern India) is the son of Shiva and Parvati. He is one of the most popular deities in Hinduism and is often found in Temples and in shrines in the home.

The elephant head could be a symbol of the wisdom of God but there are various stories as to how he actually came to get an elephant's head. Here are two popular accounts:

a) When Ganesha was born, Parvati was so proud of him that she invited all the gods to come and admire him. Unfortunately, she inadvertently invited Sari, the evil one who burnt Ganesha's head to ashes as soon as he looked upon the baby. Brahma took pity on Parvati's grief and agreed to replace the baby's head with that of the first living creature that came by - it was an elephant!

b) Parvati decided to have a bath and told Ganesha not to let anyone enter the house. Shiva, on returning home, could not get by his single-minded son and decapitated him in a fit of outrage. Parvati was naturally overcome with grief and Shiva remorsefully agreed to replace the babies head with that of the first living creature to come by. Again, it was an elephant.

Ganesha's popularity is also due to the fact that he is the remover of obstacles. He is therefore prayed to whenever someone starts a new project such as beginning a new job, getting married, learning to drive a car, buying a house and so on.

In one hand Ganesha holds a goad which is an instrument for guiding elephants. In another he holds a noose for catching wild elephants. The third hand holds a dish of sweets which he is sniffing with his trunk! The fourth hand is held in a gesture which means "Do not be afraid"

Finally, his companion is a rat. This represents the fact that Ganesha is a friend of all living creatures, even those that are despised by the majority.

Activities

1 Pupils could visit a Hindu Temple or Mandir to see how Ganesha is portrayed and revered.

2 Pupils may wish to draw a picture of Ganesha and label the symbols associated with him.

3 Pupils could read about how Ganesha received the head of an elephant. They could then design a cartoon which brings out the main features of the story.

Hindu worship

Puja tray set out for worship

Hindu homes will often have an area set aside for daily worship or puja. Puja is actually the offerings that are made to the deity as part of a Hindu's prayer. Often these offerings are presented on a Puja tray as pictured here. The offerings may be of food (rice, nuts, sweets, fruit, milk) or flowers, incense and so on.

The objects on the puja tray are:

• **a bell** which is rung at the beginning of puja to alert the deity that worship is about to commence.

• **a small water pot (lota)** which contains the water symbolising cleansing and purification.

• **a spoon** used to offer the water (or milk) to the deity and to the devotees.

• **a diva or arti lamp.** This is filled with ghee (clarified butter) and usually has five wicks made of cotton wool which burn throughout puja.

The naked flame is an important element in Hindu worship and symbolises the enlightenment of the soul and the removal of the darkness of ignorance. It is also a symbol of the presence of God.

• **an incense burner.** Incense is burnt to create an aroma pleasing to the deity.

• **a dish.** This contains sandalwood paste and is used to mark the forehead of the devotee. This is known as a tilak mark and it is a sign of God's blessing.

The puja tray and all the utensils are made of steel which signifies purity. All the food, after being offered to the deity is then consumed by the devotee. By accepting the food, which is known as Prashad, the worshipper shows that he or she accepts the blessings of the deity.

During puja, all the five senses are involved and this is not accidental, it shows that in Hindu puja, the whole person is completely taken up in worship.

Also all four elements of earth, water, fire and air are used in worship: the fruits of the earth, a bowl of water, the naked flame and incense to perfume the air.

While the offerings are made, prayers are said such as verses from the Vedas.

Activities

1 If Hindu children are present, they may wish to demonstrate what they do at puja, while the rest of the class observes.

2 Ask your pupils to identify the five senses and indicate how they are all involved during puja.

3 Ask your pupils to draw each of the items placed on the puja tray and to label them. They could also explain the significance of each item.

Weddings

A Hindu wedding garland made of sandalwood, with dolls.

This is a delightful artefact because of its rich sandalwood smell! It really is an opportunity for pupils to become involved through using their senses.

The Hindu wedding, like most weddings is very much a social occasion. It is not just the joining together of a man and a woman but also the coming together of two families.

It is a very colourful occasion where the bride and groom dress in special clothes. The bride usually dresses in a red sari and the groom is adorned with a garland such as the one pictured here, or one made with real flowers.

The couple are married under a wedding canopy which is festooned with tinsel, flowers and pictures of various deities. As mentioned before on page 107, Ganesha is very much in evidence during the wedding ceremony.

The couple, wearing cords around their necks, sit facing one another under the canopy and are sprinkled with rice. Towards the end of the ceremony a fire is lit and the bride and groom walk seven steps around it. At each step a special request is made for their future happiness and prosperity. The end of the ceremony is marked by the bride and groom giving one another some rice to eat. This signifies that they will now have to look after one another. Finally tilak marks are put on each of their foreheads as a sign of God's blessing and it is time for photographs to be taken and for food.

Activities

1 Let the children smell the garland. Ask them what the smell reminds them of. Some questions might be: What does a sweet smell represent? Why should a sweet smell be associated with a wedding?

2 Pupils may wish to find out more about a Hindu wedding. Older pupils could compare the Hindu wedding ceremony with a Jewish or Christian wedding. What are the similarities and the main differences?

3 Students could make up their own wishes for a bride and groom, before finding out what Hindus ask for at the seven steps around the sacred fire.

Mendhi patterns

(For a photograph of Henna paste and a stencil for Mendhi patterns, see page 93.)

These artefacts have more of a cultural than a religious significance. In fact they are used by Hindus, Moslems and Christians in India and Pakistan.

Here we are concerned about their use in a Hindu context where they are used particularly at Hindu weddings and during the festival of Divali.

The Henna paste is applied onto the hands and

the feet. When it is washed off it leaves a brown dye which lasts for about a week. The henna is applied so as to make intricate patterns which are known as Mendhi or Mehandi patterns. Stencils allow the making of the pattern so much easier and less time consuming. Here is a typical Mendhi pattern.

Activities

1 Ask the pupils to find out about what happens at a Hindu wedding. Videos are also available for pupils to watch and make their own notes.

2 Pupils can design their own Mendhi patterns and try them out on their friends. Henna is fairly cheap to buy and readily available from Asian retailers but you may prefer to use poster paints.

Divali

Divali is a popular New Year festival which lasts for two to five days. It takes place in the Autumn and is closely associated with the goddess Lakshmi (see page 99). As Lakshmi is the goddess of wealth and prosperity, Divali is a time for people to straighten their financial affairs, such as settle any outstanding debts.

Divali cards are sent to friends and relatives wishing them a happy Divali.

Diva lamps

Diva lamps are filled with ghee (clarified butter) with cotton wicks floating on the surface. These are lit and the lamps are placed in windows or outside doors in order to attract Lakshmi. The hope is that she will visit their homes and bless them with prosperity for the coming New Year.

Activities

1 Pupils can design their own Divali cards to make a display or to send to their Hindu friends.

2 The symbol of light is prominent in the festival of Divali. Pupils could explore their own feelings of light and darkness and respond through creative writing, music, art. movement and dance.

3 Older pupils could compare the three festivals of Divali, Hanukah and Christmas. They could explore the way the symbol of light is used in very different ways in each of these festivals.

Hindu comics

The pictures here show just a small selection of Hindu comics which are available in this country. They are extremely popular, not just with children but also with adults! They also provide an enjoyable way for non-Hindus to learn something about the Hindu religion.

The topics covered by the comics include extracts from the Great epics such as the Mahabharata and the Ramayana, the Bhagavad Gita and the Vedas. Some of these writings can be rather difficult to delve into, whereas the comics provide a fairly easy entry. They also touch upon the different deities and even famous personalities such as Ramakrishna and Gandhi.

Activities

1 Let the children read and enjoy some of the comics. It may be interesting to compare them with some of our modern secular comics and also with Christian comics about biblical themes.

2 Pupils may wish to design their own comics about religious and ethical themes.

OM

A badge depicting the symbol OM

OM is also an important element in birth ceremonies. When a baby is born, the symbol OM is traced on the baby's tongue with honey.

Activities

1 Pupils could write out the verse from the Upanishad and then super-impose the symbol OM over the writing using light coloured pencils.

2 Pupils could find out more about what happens during the Hindu birth ceremony.

The badge shown here contains the main symbol of Hinduism which is known as OM or AUM.

Om is a mantra, a chant which is repeated as an aid to meditation in Yoga. Om is believed to be the sacred syllable, which was the first sound which brought about the whole of creation.

Here is a references to OM in the Upanishads:

That word which all the Vedas declare, which all the austerities proclaim, for which people live the life of a religious student, that word, I will tell you, is brief. That is AUM.

Kathupanishad 1.2.15

Buddhist artefacts

Contents

Introduction to Buddhist Iconography

There are many different representations of the Buddha, which reflect the different concerns of Mahayana and Theravada Buddhism. In turn, both of these use different styles, depending upon the country of origin. There is one unifying factor, however: each different statue of the Buddha has something fundamental to show us about Buddhist teaching.

The weath of symbolism in some Buddhist images can be confusing. For this reason, some simplified line drawings are used in this chapter, illustrating features depicted in many different styles in actual Buddhist artefacts.

One of the most important artistic devices used in both traditions is the employment of mudras. These have their origins in Hinduism. Mudras are different hand gestures which are used in Buddhist art to depict the different qualities of the Enlightened Mind. The five most popular mudras used in Buddhist art are:

Bhumisparsa-mudra

Literally "earth-touching". Buddha, on receiving enlightenment, called upon the earth to witness to this event.

Varada-mudra

This is a gesture of compassion and giving.

Dhyana-mudra

This represents total concentration in meditation.

Buddhas

Abhaya-mudra

The upraised palm signifies protection and reassurance. The left hand remains in the dhyana mudra.

The following images of Buddha are to be found within Mahayana Buddhism and represent different aspects of Buddhahood. They also convey different aspects of the wisdom of Enlightenment.

Buddha Akshobya

Vitarka-mudra

This depicts teaching Buddhist doctrine and reasoning.

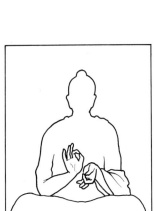

A statué which shows the Bhumisparsa mudra.

The Akshobya Buddha is depicted as deep blue in colour. He is seated upon an "elephant throne" which gives a hint as to the meaning of Akshobya: "unshakeable" and "immovable". Notice he is holding a vajra (see page 123). The particular aspect of wisdom that he portrays is that of "The Mirror", reflecting the true nature of reality.

Buddha Ratnasambhava

Buddha Amitabha

The Ratnasambhava Buddha is depicted as golden yellow in colour. He is holding a jewel in the palm of his hand and this reflects the meaning of his name "Jewel producing". The jewel represents the Three Jewels which are:

1 The Buddha - the Enlightened One

2 The Dharma - the teaching of the Buddha

3 The Sangha - the disciples or community who live out the teachings of the Buddha.

He is seated upon a "windhorse throne". The windhorse is found in Tibetan art which shows it carrying the Three Jewels upon its back. It is bright white, as a symbol of purity and also, as a galloping horse, it demonstrates the joy and pleasure to be found in spiritual practice.

The aspect of wisdom that he portrays is that of "Equality".

The Amitabha Buddha is depicted as deep red like the sunset. His name means "Infinite Light". He is seen here, holding a lotus flower which is a Hindu symbol but has a different significance for Buddhists: just as the lotus emerges fresh and clean from out of the dirty water, so too the Enlightened Mind remains untouched and untroubled amidst the transient world. The lotus also signifies spiritual rebirth and growth.

He is seated upon a peacock-throne. Not only is the peacock an elegant bird, but it is also said to be capable of eating poisonous snakes and is used as a symbol here for the transforming power of meditation. The aspect of wisdom portrayed here is that of "Discriminating Awareness"

Buddha Amoghasiddhi

Buddha Vairocana.

The Amoghasiddhi Buddha is deep green in colour and the name means "Infallible Success". His throne is of Shang-shangs which are creatures half human and half bird. They symbolise the nature of Amoghasiddhi Buddha who unites opposites. He is also shown holding a double vajra (see page. 123). The particular aspect of wisdom portrayed here is that of "Success in Spiritual Endeavour".

The Vairocana Buddha is bright white so as to depict the colour of the midday sun. His name means "The Illuminator". He sits upon a throne of lions to depict the authority of Enlightenment. His emblem is the eight spoked wheel of the Dharma or way of Enlightenment (eight spokes represent the eightfold path). This Buddha expresses the idea that the Dharms (teaching) is made available to all, and can lead everyone to enlightenment..

Activities

1 Before pupils investigate the significance of the statue they have in front of them, they could explore their own responses such as: how does it make them feel? Do they like it? They could then make suggestions as to what particular aspect of Buddhism they think the statue is trying to convey.

2 Pupils could identify which particular mudra is being used in each of the statues. Does this contribute to their appreciation of the statue?

3 Colour is an important aspect of the statues described here. Pupils could explore this use of colour and elsewhere in religious expression.

4 Pupils might be able to visit a Buddhist Shrine and photograph or draw the different images of Buddha found there. They could also explore the way puja (worship and ceremony) is conducted at the shrine and take note of the rich variety of symbols within the shrine.

Bodhisattvas

Apart from different Buddhas, you may also come across images of Bodhisattvas (literally, 'Bodhi-beings', or 'enlightenment beings'). These represent aspects of the path to enlightenment - e.g. wisdom, compassion, insight. They are not representations of the historical Buddha (Sakyamuni) but symbolise enlightenment in an ideal form.

In Theravada Buddhism there are only two Bodhisattvas:

1. Previous incarnations of the historical Buddha, during which Buddhists believe he developed and perfected qualities that led him to enlightenme.nt.

2. A future Buddha known as Maitreya who is believed come to earth in the future to restore the Dharma (the teachings of the Buddha)

Mahayana Buddhists on the other hand recognise many Bodhisattvas whose images help men and women who seek enlightenment. Here are three of the most popular:

A postcard of Avalokiteshvara

Avalokiteshvara

Avalokiteshvara (or Avalokita) is the most popular of the Bodhisattvas. He is usually shown sitting on a lotus throne and is called 'The Jewell in the Lotus'. He represents compassion, a central feature of enlightenment, and is often referred to (strictly incorrectly, since he is a Bodhisattva rather than a Buddha) as 'The Buddha of Compassion'. Some images of him have many arms, indicating that he is helping everywhere. Others show him stepping down from the lotus throne, indicating that he enters into the world of suffering in order to show compassion.

Avalokiteshvara is particularly popular in Tibetan Buddhism. The Dalai Lama is regarded as an incarnation of this bodhisattva. His mantra (a set of words which symbolise him, and may be chanted in worship) is OM MANI PADME HUM. This expresses the idea of spiritual treasure(MANI) being in the lotus (the lotus - PADME -referring to the lotus throne, and also to the process of human enlightenment).

Manjugosha

Manjugosha or Manjushri is the Bodhisattva of wisdom. He is depicted as a young prince with the sword of wisdom in one hand and the book of the Dharma in the other. His youthfulness is a symbol for the energy and vitality that the wisdom of enlightenment brings. Often he is seated on a blue lotus and his body is golden orange in colour.

Poster of Manjugosha (Manjushri)

Tara

Tara is female and represents the compassionate attribute of enlightenment. She is deep green in colour and surrounded by a rainbow halo. She is depicted as a beautiful princess, dressed in the finest of silk robes. At the same time she is not remote; although she is seated in the posture of meditation, she is stepping down with one foot. This symbolises her readiness to help all those in need.

According to Buddhist legend, Tara was born out of the tears shed by Avalokiteshvara when he saw the sufferings of the world, therefore she shares some of his features.

A poster of Tara

Vajrapani

Vajrapani

Vajrapani, in many ways bears some
resemblance to the Hindu deity, Shiva Nataraja
(see page 24), in the way he is portrayed. He is
the Bodhisattva of spiritual power and energy.
No obstacle can prevent him from reaching
enlightenment. He is of a powerful build and
blue in colour. He wields a vajra in one hand and
dresses in a tiger skin with a garland of skulls in
his hair. His halo is made up of flames.

Activities

1 Pupils could examine some of the symbols used to
portray these (and other) Bodhisattvas. They raise some

interesting questions such as:

- why should a sword represent wisdom?

- why are different colours used for the Bodhisattvas?

2 Pupils could compare the similarities between Shiva
Nataraj and Vajrapani. Also, are there any significant
differences?

Siddharta Gautama

This drawing on the opposite page shows
Siddhartha Gautama before he became the
Buddha. After leaving his sheltered and princely
life, he wandered through the forest in his
search for meaning. He met some Hindu
ascetics who taught him that salvation (moksha)
would only come through total self denial. He
therefore gave up all earthly pleasures and
fasted until he was almost a skeleton. The story
goes (and children love this!) that he became so
thin that when he put his finger in his navel, he
could feel his back-bone. However, he soon
realised that the ascetic life was not going to
bring him salvation, only death. He therefore
began eating again and set off, stronger and
more determined, to discover the key to
enlightenment.

As we know Siddhartha Gautama became the
Buddha, which means the "Enlightened One"
and began to preach a Middle Way which
rejected both asceticism and luxurious living. His
first converts were the Hindu ascetics whom he
had met in the forest. This image of Siddhartha
the ascetic, then, is a reminder of his early life
and the subsequent balance he found through
the Middle Way.

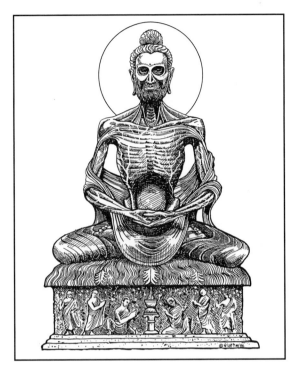

An image of Siddhartha Gautama as an ascetic, before his experience of enlightenment.

Activities

1 Children enjoy the story of Siddhartha's childhood, marriage and quest for enlightenment. They can research the story and make a display of the significant moments in his life. They could also make masks and re-enact the main events.

2 Pupils may like to investigate what Buddha's Middle Way actually means. This would entail an investigation into the Four Noble Truths and the Eightfold Path.

3 Older children can investigate the place asceticism plays (or has played) in religion today. For example the place of fasting in religion.

Meditation

Although meditation itself requires no artefacts, we illustrate here three popular aids to meditation used particularly in Tibetan Buddhism.

Mandalas

Mandala is a sanscrit word meaning "circle" or "centre". They are often highly intricate circular geometric patterns which are used as an aid to concentration by certain Mahayana Buddhists, in particular in Tibet. They can be painted, made of different coloured grains, sands or even modelled in 3-D. The stupas which house relics of the Buddha, for example, are three dimensional mandalas.

Mandalas are often very colourful and the colours themselves are symbols for the different qualities of the Buddha: white represents his purity, red represents his compassion and blue represents the vastness and truth of his teachings.

The mandala is essentially a vehicle for concentrating the mind of the meditator. The idea is for the mind to shake off its usual fetters and to enter into the mandala. The centre represents Absolute Truth and it is the ultimate goal for the meditator. He or she has to internalise the mandala and therefore by exploring the various aspects and dimensions within the mandala pattern, begin to explore themselves. Many mandalas are made up of a series of concentric circles where each ring symbolises a particular attribute or step that the meditator must pass through in order to progress. Sometimes the mandala may be made up of a square or squares within a circle. The square is intended to represent the earth.

The following symbols are often used:

- The flames on the outer ring represent the negative wordly concerns that have to be burnt up before entering into the spiritual reality of the mandala.

- The ring of vajras symbolises the determination needed by the meditator in order to progress.

- The cremation grounds are a popular Buddhist symbol and represent the spiritual death and rebirth through spiritual practice.

- The gateways depicted at North, South, East and West are guarded in order to keep out negative influences.

- The lotus petals at the centre represent the purity and peace that the mind finds through meditation.

Activities

1 Many objects in the natural world resemble the mandala. For example: the eye itself; a snowflake crystal; some flowers...Also man-made objects sometimes remind us of the mandala (rose window, maze, buildings..). Pupils could think about this as a class and draw up a larger list.

2 Some pupils might like to design their own mandalas and display them.

3 Older pupils could read about how C.G Jung used andalas as a therapeutic device with his patients in his autobiography "Memories, Dreams and Reflections" and "The Secret of the Golden Flower".

The Wheel of Life

A poster of the Wheel of Life

The wheel of life is an excellent means for older pupils to investigate Buddhist teachings and philosophy. It can be purchased either as a wall hanging, known as a thanka, or more easily as a poster. It represents the Buddhist teachings on the suffering and impermanence of existence., and is rich in symbolism:

The demonic figure holding the wheel of life is Yama who is the Lord of death. He is devouring the wheel and therefore all existence. In simple terms he personifies death and therefore the impermanence of all life.

The theme of impermanence is also symbolised within the centre of the wheel which depicts three animals endlessly chasing and biting each other's tails. The red cock represents passion and lust, the green snake represents hatred and aggression and the black pig stands for ignorance and confusion.

The next circle depicts beings which either rise into the three higher realms or sink into the three lower regions. These six realms are then illustrated within the next circle which make up the six spokes of the wheel. They are:

1 the hell realm (lower part of wheel) which is characterised by extreme sufferings such as hot and cold,

2 the hungry ghost realm (lower left) characterised by insatiable hunger,

3 the animal realm (lower right) characterised by extreme stupidity,

4 the jealous gods realm (upper left) characterised by competitiveness and ambition,

5 the god realm (top) characterised by a picture of a sensual heaven and the pursuit of pleasure,

6 the human realm (upper right). It is only this realm, with its constant fluctuation between pleasure and pain, that offers the path to enlightenment.

In the outer ring there are twelve figures which represent a chain of cause and effect which perpetuates the endless cycle of rebirth and therefore impedes enlightenment.

The twelve figures (starting at the top and then following around in a clockwise direction) are:

1   a blind man - representing ignorance

2   a potter - action (karmic activity)

3   a monkey - consciousness

4   people in boat - name and form

5   empty house with 5 windows and a door - the six sense organs

6   sexual embrace - contact

7   man with an arrow in his eye - feeling

8   a person drinking alcohol - craving

9   a woman picking fruit from a tree - grasping

10 a pregnant woman - becoming

11 a child being born - rebirth

12 an old person and a corpse - old age and death

Finally, on either side of Yama's head there are two scenes. on the right is depicted the paradise of Amitabha (see page 116) and on the left is Sakyamuni Buddha (the name given to the historical Buddha, Siddhartha Gautama) who has escaped from the wheel of existence and now points to the perfect wheel, the Buddhadharma which is the most popular symbol for Buddhism.

The Wheel of Life is a spiritual map, upon which the Buddhist can trace his or her progress towards enlightenment, and be warned of the consequences of certain attitudes or actions.

Activities

The "Friends of the Western Buddhist Order", together with the ILEA Teachers' Centre have produced an excellent resource pack called "Buddhist Symbols". This contains photocopy free material which includes templates of sections of the wheel of life. Pupils can piece the different templates together and make up their own wheel of life poster. This would involve a great deal of useful discussion and research into Buddhist beliefs and philosophy. The pack is now available from the South London Multifaith RE Centre, Kilmorie Road, London SE23 2SP. Tel. 081 699-0989.

Thankas

The thanka, a cloth wall-hanging,, is popular in Tibet and Bhutan. They can be vast enough to cover the outside wall of a building or small enough to hang on the wall of a Tibetan household. Sometimes they depict the wheel of life (see page 122), mandalas (see page. 121) or more often a Buddhist saint such as Padmasambhava (also known as Guru Rinpoche) who is said to have brought Buddhism to Tibet.

Thankas are used to aid meditation. For example, a Tibetan Budddhist may meditate upon a thanka with an image of Tara depicted upon it. Tara is a Bodhisattva who represents compassion (see page.119). By meditating upon her, the meditator hopes that he will develop some of the attributes of Buddha's compassion.

Thankas are fairly expensive, so a poster of a thanka may have to suffice!

Activities

1 Wisdom Publications have produced an excellent resource book on thankas called "Tara's colouring book". It contains useful information about Buddhist art in general and also black and white masters for pupils to colour in.

2 As with the "wheel of life", thankas can provide an excellent way in for older pupils to think about Buddhist beliefs and philosophy.

Worship (Puja)

Although buddhists do not worship a god or gods, puja is an opportunity to show respect for the Buddha, the Dharma (his teaching) and the Sangha (the communityof those who follow the Buddha), and to engage the body and emotions, as well as the mind, in Buddhist practice.

Tibetan Prayer Wheel

The prayer wheel is an extremely popular artefact used in Buddhism such as that practised in Tibet and Bhutan.

It is a cylindrical barrel which is either hand-held or mounted on a wall. It contains thousands of mantras such as "Om mani padme hum" which is known as the mantra of compassion. The word mantra itself means "mind protection" and the actual act of reciting a mantra or of spinning a prayer wheel reminds the individual to develop compassion and thus "protects their minds" from thoughts of aggression and ill-will. The actual spinning of the wheel is symbolic of sending out compassionate thoughts to all beings and is also a constant reminder of one of Buddha's main teachings: that all life is transitory and subject to change.

For activities and further information see page 26.

Vajra and Bell

These artefacts are associated with Tantric Buddhism which can be found in Tibet, Bhutan, Ladakh and Nepal. It began during the fourth century C.E and teaches that Enlightenment can be achieved not just here and now, but also instantaneously with just one thought or moment's inspiration.

Tantric Buddhism makes much use of ritual, mantras and mandalas (see page 121)

The vajra and the ghanta (bell) pictured here are for use in ritual and give a real flavour of Tantric Buddhism.

According to one interpretation the bell has a feminine aspect and is held in the left hand. It symbolises the wisdom that understands how all things are inter-related (just as the sound of the bell is reproduced through the inter-relation of the bell, the clapper and the bell ringer).

The vajra has a male aspect and is sometimes referred to as the "diamond thunderbolt" or the "diamond sceptre". It is held in the right hand and symbolises true compassion which should have a clarity of understanding, be multi-faceted in its concern for all and diamond-hard in its resolve to help others. By actually holding these objects, the person meditating is reminded and encouraged to develop these qualities.

Vajra and ghanta are sanscrit words. You may well come across different names such as:

	Diamond thunderbolt	bell
Sanscrit:	vajra	ghanta
Japanese:	kongosho	kenchi
Tibetan:	dorje	

Activities

1 Older pupils can investigate the particular characteristics of Tantric Buddhism.

2 Some pupils may like to do a comparitive study of the different ways in which bells are used in different religions.

Juzu beads

These prayer beads are known as Juzu beads and are used by followers of Nichiren Buddhism. This is one of the many expressions of Japanese Buddhism which has found quite a large following in the West. It was founded by Nichiren Daishonin in the 13th Century C.E.

Juzu means literally "a number of beads" and they play an important part in the daily worship of the followers of Nichiren Daishonin who said:

"Whether you chant the Buddha's name, recite the sutra, or merely offer flowers and incense, all your virtuous acts will implant benefits and good fortune in your life. With this conviction you should put your faith into practice."

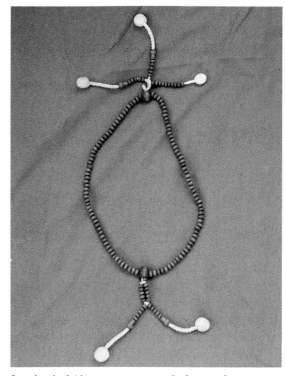

Juzu beads (laid so as to represent the human shape)

The beads are oval shaped with two tassels on one end and three on the other end. In the oval section there are 112 beads of which 108 represent the number of earthly desires, and the four smaller beads represent the four earthly Boddhisattvas. If the beads are held by the central of the three tassels they appear to have the shape of a human being.

During the chanting of "Nam-myoho-renge-kyo" which means "Glory to the Lotus Sutra", the beads are crossed over in the middle once, so that the end with three tassles is placed over the middle finger of the right hand whilst the other end is placed over the middle finger of the left hand.

Activities

1 Older pupils could find out more about Nichiren Buddhism and other Japanese Buddhist Movements such as the Rissho Kosei Kai founded by Nikkyo Niwano just after the Second World War.

2 Pupils may like to investigate the attraction of Nichiren and other expressions of Buddhism, to Western people.

Puja bowls

The offering bowls illustrated here are set before a shrine in Buddhist worship (puja). There are some similarities with Hindu puja, except, of course, the image is that of Buddha, and performance of puja is done to help the spiritual development of the worshippers, not to seek the help of a god.

Buddhist offering bowls used in puja

The various bowls are used to contain the offerings such as water, incense, flowers, rice , fruit and so on. Most Buddhist shrines will be adorned with freshly cut flowers, which apart from being beautiful, act as a reminder that all life is impermanent and subject to decay.

Activities

1 If it is possible, arrange a visit to a Buddhist shrine and ask your pupils to note what offerings are being made to the Buddha. If this is not possible, perhaps a Buddhist can come into the classroom and speak about puja.

2 In most religions there are opportunities to make offerings. It may be offerings to an image or statue or it may be a gift of money for the poor, or for the upkeep of a place of worship. Your pupils may like to carry out an investigation into the place of "giving" in different religions.

Festivals

Masks

A mask being worn for a dramatic performance at a Tibetan Buddhist festival.

Buddhist masks differ depending upon the country of origin. They are used during festivals where the whole village will join in the fun as scenes from Buddhist stories are re-enacted. (See below for celebrations at Wesak when Jataka stories are acted out by the children).

A popular Buddhist mask is that of Mara the demon who tried to tempt Siddhartha away from his quest for enlightenment. Mara, apart from being a personification of death, is also a demon who tries to block all human beings from their pursuit of Nirvana. He is therefore a significant figure in any Buddhist theatre and his appearance will serve as a warning to the people to be on their guard against spiritual complacency.

Activities

1 Pupils can make their own masks to re-enact scenes from Buddhist or other stories.

2 Pupils could find out more about how Mara tried to tempt Siddhartha away from his quest for enlightenment.

Wesak

Wesak (Vesak) is one of the most popular festivals in Theravada Buddhism. It takes place in April/May during a full moon. Wesak celebrates the birth, the Enlightenment and the entry into Parinirvana (death) of the Buddha, which according to Theravada Buddhists, all took place on the same day of the year. Mahayana Buddhists celebrate the birth and death of the Buddha on different occasions, but still celebrate his enlightenment at Wesak..

In Sri Lanka, which is an important centre for Theravada Buddhism, Wesak (or Vesaka) Puja is celebrated with offerings of lotus blossom and incense. Also lanterns are made and torchlight processions are held. Light is an important symbol in this festival and represents the light or enlightenment which the Buddha received. It also represents the light which Buddha's disciples can obtain if they follow his teachings.

Children in Sri Lanka also act out moral stories which are known as "Jataka" stories. They are about the previous lives of the Buddha and often contain animals within the plot. Some of these can be found in childrens' collections of stories such as the "talkative tortoise" which is about a tortoise being carried in the air by two geese. He grips a stick in his mouth so that the geese can carry him. Unfortunately, when some children taunt him he answers back and falls to his death!

Activities

1 Your pupils could design their own Wesak cards which depict scenes from the birth, Enlightenment and death of the Buddha.

2 Pupils could design and make their own Wesak paper lanterns.

3 Pupils could read more of the Jataka stories and act them out. They might like to combine this with the making of Buddhist masks.

Sikh artefacts

Contents

The 5 K's

Sikhs wear five symbols as a sign of their faith. These are known as the 5 K's as they all begin with the letter K in Punjabi. Both men and women wear the same symbols as both sexes enjoy equal rights in Sikh religion.

The five K's are: Kesh, Kirpan, Kaccha, Kangha and Kara and are described below.

Kesh

The first K is Kesh which means uncut hair on the head and the face. The turban itself is not one of the five K's but is worn simply to keep the uncut hair clean. A male Sikh makes a knot with his long hair on the top of his head and covers it with a turban or pagri in Punjabi. Boys start wearing turbans at about the age of seven when their hair is long enough. The first turban will be tied by the Granthi or by an elder from the Sikh community. This ceremony is carried out in the presence of the Sikh Holy book (the Guru Granth Sahib) and with the family and friends. Before the age of seven boys will simply wear their hair tied in a top knot and covered with a Patka (a square piece of cloth about the size of a handkerchief). Turban cloth is easily available and is surprisingly long: about 5 metres. Actually tying a turban takes a great deal of skill and practice and is illustrated here. You may also see Sikh men wearing a net simply to keep their beards tidy and clean.

Women do not wear turbans but a dupatta which is a kind of scarf worn around the shoulders and head.

Examining a turban length in the classroom.

Kangha

The Kangha is simply a comb in order to keep the hair in place before the turban is tied. It is usually made of wood or ivory but can also be made of other materials such as plastic. Notice the tiny metal emblem on the side of one of the Kanghas illustrated here. For more information on this see under Kirpan.

Kara

The Kara or bangle/bracelet is made of steel and is worn on the wrist of the right hand. It is not an ornament but is worn to remind the wearer of his or her unity with God and of the Khalsa brotherhood. It is loose fitting so that it moves when the believer is using his or her hand - a reminder always to do good with one's hands.

Kirpan

The Kirpan or sword/dagger is a reminder that once the Sikhs were warriors. Now, however, the war is more of a spiritual battle and the Kirpan has become a symbol of honour, dignity, bravery and self sacrifice. It is made of steel and is usually about 20cms long. It reminds the wearer to defend the weak and uphold the truth.

Some Sikhs will wear a Kirpan as illustrated here, on a sling underneath their clothes, whilst many in Britain will wear a Kirpan badge or tie pin. The metal emblem on the Kangha is in fact a miniature Kirpan which shows just how much the sword has become a symbol for Sikhs living in Britain today.

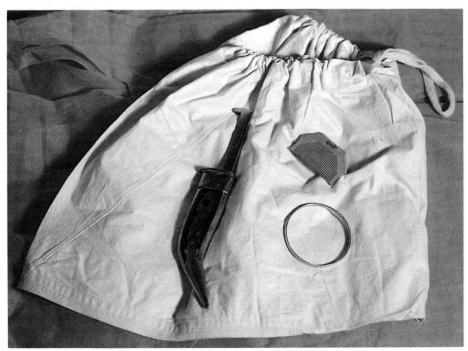

A kangha, kara, kirpan and kaccha

Kaccha

All baptised Sikhs, men and women, wear the Kaccha or shorts as undergarments. They used to be knee-length when they were originally introduced by the Guru. They were introduced for practical reasons. They gave much more freedom of movement in battle than the dhoti which was previously worn.

N.B. Sikhs for understandable reasons are not happy for this artefact to be shown in the classroom. Therefore it is better to simply make a pattern of the Kaccha for illustrative purposes.

Activities

1 If you have the opportunity invite Sikhs into the classroom to talk about what the 5 K's mean to them. They may even be willing to demonstrate how to tie a turban or wear a dupatta.
Some questions to ask a Sikh visitor might be:
Why are so many Sikh artefacts made of steel? What difficulties do young Sikhs encounter living here in Britain?

2 Pupils may like to examine the Kara and think about the use of the unbroken circle as a symbol. They may like to think of similar symbols such as a wedding or signet ring.

3 If you are able to purchase a Kangha with the miniature Kirpan on the side, ask pupils to try to work out what it represents.

4 Pupils may be able to carry out an investigation about police training with regards to carrying the Kirpan in this country and training of the medical profession with regard to the wearing of the Kaccha.

5 Older pupils might like to explore some of the issues which Sikhs encounter in practising their religion in Britain today. Role play might provide a useful vehicle for empathetic work in this area.

The Gurus

This plaque depicts the founder of the Sikh religion, Guru Nanak, who was born in 1469 CE. The word Guru means teacher.

There are many books about his life which are accessible to children and therefore we will not devote space to him here except to say that he drew upon his experiences of Hinduism and Islam in his search for Truth. He discovered that God is within each person and called God "Sat Guru" (the True Guru) and also "Nam" which means simply "Name". When asked to describe God he used these words:

"There is One God. Eternal Truth is His name: Maker of all things, Timeless is His image. He is not begotten, He is self-existent. By the grace of the Guru He is made known to men."

After Guru Nanak there were nine more Gurus. It is important to note that the Gurus are not worshipped by Sikhs, but held in high esteem as messengers of God.

The ten gurus

Guru Nanak	1469-1539
Guru Angad	1504-1552
Guru Amar Das	1479-1574
Guru Ram Das	1534-1581
Guru Arjan	1563-1606
Guru Har Gobind	1595-1646
Guru Har Rai	1630-1661
Guru Har Krishen	1656-1664
Guru Tegh Bahadur	1621-1675
Guru Gobind Singh	1666-1708

Guru Har Krishen was only five when he became a Guru and died of chicken-pox at the age of eight

Guru Gobind Singh

After Guru Nanak the most well known Guru was Guru Gobind Singh. Again, details of his life are readily available elsewhere. All that needs to be said is that Guru Gobind Singh as the last Guru established the Khalsa or Brotherhood of Sikhs in a dramatic ceremony. He also commanded all Sikhs to wear the five symbols known as the five K's and declared that there would be no more human Gurus after his death.

The writings of the Adi Granth were rewritten and named by Guru Gobind Singh as the Guru Granth Sahib. These writings contained the teachings of the first five and the ninth Gurus and would now be regarded as the living Guru for all time.

Guru Gobind Singh

Activities

1 Pupils could read about the life of Guru Nanak and make a wall display to bring out the most significant events in his life and to illustrate some of his teachings.

2 It may be possible to invite a Sikh into the classroom who could talk about the ten Gurus. Otherwise pupils could carry out their own research in order to draw out the main contributions of each Guru.

3 Further reading could be about Guru Gobind Singh and the foundation of the Khalsa when he asked for the heads of five true Sikhs.

Sikh Initiation

When he founded the Khalsa or Brotherhood of Sikhs, Guru Gobind Singh also introduced an initiation rite, known as the Amrit ceremony, to the Sikh religion. This is still practised today and marks an important stage in the life of a Sikh.

Bata and patashas

Amrit is a sweet water which can be made by dissolving sugar lumps or patashas in water. This is stirred by five elders (the five beloved ones) using the Khanda or double edged sword. The Amrit is then drunk by each of those being initiated and also sprinkled into their eyes and upon their uncut hair. The men are given the name of Singh (lion) and the women are named Kaur (princess). The drink from the shared bowl of Amrit is significant. It was deliberately introduced by Guru Gobind Singh to show that Sikhs rejected the Hindu caste system.

The Khanda, because it has a ceremonial use, is not an easy artefact to find. The bowl and the packet of patashas are, however, easier to obtain. The bowl is a more functional object and is also used to keep the Karah Parshad (see Activities below). A bowl and kirpan are shown on the back cover of this book.

If patashas is not available, sugar cubes will make an ideal substitute as they need encouragement in order to dissolve.

Activities

1 Pupils could act out the dramatic ceremony in which Guru Gobind Singh founded the Khalsa Brotherhood.

2 Pupils might explore features of Sikh initiation by asking questions such as:
What is the significance of sugared water in the ceremony?
Why is the Amrit sprinkled upon the uncut hair and into the eyes?
What is the significance of the titles "lion" and "princess"?

3 A Sikh visitor who has been initiated might be able to describe what the ceremony really meant to him or her and how it has affected his or her life.

4 Sikhs sometimes describe the Amrit ceremony as Sikh baptism. Pupils might compare adult or believers baptism (eg within the Baptist Church) with Sikh baptism and explore some of the beliefs behind these two ceremonies.

Steel bowl and khanda.

5 The steel bowl (bata) is also used to keep the Karah Parshad which is given out to all at the end of Sikh worship. It is simply food which has been blessed by God and, like the shared Amrit, signifies a rejection of the Hindu caste system by stating that all people are equal in the sight of God. Pupils could consider the importance of food within Sikhism, a study which could be enriched by a visit to a Gurdwara so that pupils can see the cooking and dining facilities which are an integral part of the Gurdwara.

6 Some pupils might like to make their own Karah Parshad. Here is a typical recipe:

Karah Parshad

Equal quantities of Flour ,Sugar, Water and Ghee (clarified butter)

- Add the melted ghee to the flour and cook over a low heat until brown.

- Disolve the sugar in boiling water and gradually add to the mixture.

- Cook, stirring all the time until the mixture leaves the side of the pan.

- Leave to cool before serving.

Beliefs

Khanda

The Sikh emblem is known as the Khanda, which in itself contains three symbols, the double edged sword, the circle and the pair of kirpans. For further information, see pages 28 and 29.

The central symbol is the double edged sword which is also known as the Khanda. It is not an easy artefact to find as it has a ceremonial use in the Gurdwara (the Sikh place of worship). For more information see under Sikh Initiation.

The Khanda is often found in the form of a badge or on a pennant. Outside the Sikh Gurdwara a saffron coloured flag will often be seen with the Khanda clearly marked upon it.

Activities

1 Pupils could draw the Khanda, the Sikh emblem. They may wish to make each part of the emblem on separate pieces of card so that the three symbols can be easily identified. This would involve making three templates: one for the two Kirpans, one for the Khanda and one for the Chakkar.

2 If pupils live close to a Gurdwara, they might be able to visit and photograph the different ways the Khanda is used as an emblem or badge.

3 Pupils could make a wall display of the central symbols used by the main world religions.

'Ik Onkar' badge

The badge illustrated here contains a design known as the "Ik onkar". It is simply Punjabi for the statement of faith "There is only one God", which is the first phrase of the Mool Mantra, a hymn composed by Guru Nanak. This mantra is considered to be so fundamental that it appears at the beginning of every chapter in the Guru Granth Sahib. It states:

"There is only one God
Truth is his name
He is the creator
He is without fear
He is without hate
He is timeless and without form
He is beyond death, the enlightened one
He can be known by the Guru's grace."

The Ik onkar can also be found on romalla cloths (see opposite) and often on the canopy above the Guru Granth Sahib.

Activities

1 If pupils are able to visit a gurdwara, they could look out for the Ik onkar.

2 Older pupils could examine Sikh belief about God through a study of the Mool Mantra. They could also compare this Sikh statement of faith with statements of faith from Judaism (the Shema), Islam (the first pillar) and Christianity (the Nicene Creed).

Worship

Chauri

The chauri is used when reading from the Sacred Writings which are known as the Guru Granth Sahib. The chauri is waved periodically over the book and was obviously necessary in hot countries in order to keep the flies from settling on the sacred pages. Here in England however, the chauri has more of a symbolic function. There are not so many flies and the

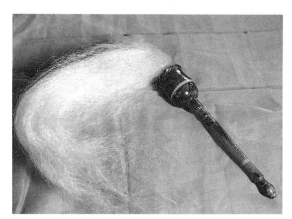

This chauri is made of Yak's hair which is embedded into a wooden handle. Some chauris may be ornately carved.

waving of the chauri reminds Sikhs of the sacred quality of the Guru Granth Sahib. It also reminds the faithful that their scriptures are alive and should be treated as a living Guru.

Romalla cloths

These ornate cloths are used to cover the Guru Granth Sahib when it is not being read. They are often decorated with Sikh symbols.

The romalla cloths are often donated by members of the congregation as a mark of respect for the sacred writings. Apart from keeping the Scriptures clean, they are, as clothes, a reminder that the Guru Granth Sahib is a living Guru.

A romalla cloth

Mala

The beads illustrated here are used by Sikhs as an aid to prayer in a similar way to most prayer beads. The usual custom is to repeat the phrase "Waha Guru" which means "God is Great". There are 108 beads.

Nit Nem

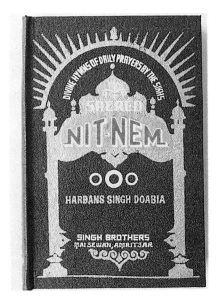

The Nit Nem is a book of sacred songs or hymns which are used daily in the home and in the Gurdwara.

Below is an extract from a sikh hymn

> **God is the Fountain of truth, intelligence, peace and pleasure and can destroy all.**
>
> **None is bigger than God, Who is the cause of worldly beauties and is present everywhere.**
>
> **God is the giver of Spiritual power and He confers true wisdom and success.**
>
> **God is the biggest Master and nurses all, without being seen.**
>
> **God gives success and mental power, and is the Fountain of pity.**
>
> **God cannot be harmed or destroyed by anybody and He has no name or desire.**
>
> **God is the conqueror of all and is present everywhere and in all living beings.**

Activities

1 Pupils could make their own replica of a chauri. Perhaps they could make their own choices about the design and the materials which they will use.

2 The chauri and the romalla cloths reveal the Sikh belief that the Guru Granth Sahib is a living Guru. Pupils might be able to research into other Sikh practices which reinforce this attitude to the Scriptures. They may also be able to compare the way other religions treat their sacred writings (for example the Jewish Torah).

3 Prayer beads are used by certain groups within most religions. Pupils may be able to compare the way prayer beads are used by some Christians, Muslims, Buddhists and Sikhs and what prayers are said by the adherents.

2 It may be possible to find a recording of Sikh devotional songs and to play it to the class.

5 If pupils have access to a Nit Nem, ask them to choose a song which interests them and explain to their peers why they have made that particular choice.

Amritsar

A wall hanging depicting the Golden Temple in Amritsar

Decorations showing the Golden Temple at Amritsar

Many Sikh homes will have ornaments or wall-hangings depicting Guru Nanak, or as shown here, a scene of the Golden Temple of Amritsar. Guru Arjan is said to have built the first Gurdwara at Amritsar. The Golden Temple (Harmandir), however, was built about 1801 and is an important site for Sikhs all over the world.

The name Amritsar itself means "pool of nectar" as the Golden Temple is built in the middle of a lake which is reported to have waters with miraculous healing properties.

Activities

1 Pupils could find where Amritsar is located in an atlas and draw a map as part of a wall display.

2 They may draw a picture of the Golden Temple and perhaps even make a model of it.

3 Pupils could find out whether or not pilgrimage to Amritsar is an important aspect of Sikh religion. For your own information, Sikhs do not place any importance in pilgrimages.

Appendix - Artefact Boxes

The following suggestions are for making up basic boxes of artefacts on the six religions covered in this book. Approximate prices are given.

Judaism Box

Cards for Bar Mitzvah and Bat Mitzvah	£1.00
Cards for Passover and Rosh Hashanah	£1.00
Skull cap	£2.00
Prayer shawl (small)	£10.00
Chanukkah candlestick	£12.00
Havdalah candle	£1.00
Havdalah spice-box	£5.00
Seder plate	£8.00
Mezuzah case	£5.00
TOTAL	£45.00

(Make a matzah cover and challah cover. Use a white table-cloth for display.)

Christianity Box

Paschal candle with transfer	£ 4.00
Baptism candle	£ 1.00
Rosary beads	£ 2.50
Holy water stoup	£ 1.00
Advent calendar	£ 1.00
Advent candle	£ 1.50
Cross	£ 2.00
Crucifix	£ 4.00
Cards for Christening, dedication, believer's baptism, first communion, confirmation and church wedding.	£ 3.00
TOTAL:	£20.00

(Ask other teachers to save you some Christmas and Easter cards. Include one of the school Bibles and a separate New Testament. Ask at your local church for a few small wafers, a priest's wafer and possibly a palm cross. Use any goblet for a chalice.)

Islam Box

Prayer mat with compass	£10.00
Holy Qur'an	£ 7.00
Muslim book stand	£ 3.00
Prayer cap	£ 1.00
Prayer beads	£ 2.00
Postcards/ festival cards	£ 2.00
TOTAL:	£25.00

(Use a clean square of material to wrap up the Qur'an, and look out for green cloths to use for drapes in display.)

Hinduism Box

Plastic image	£ 5.00
Poster of deity	£ 1.00
Puja set	£12.00
Joss sticks	50
Clay diva	£ 1.00
2 Divali cards	50
TOTAL:	£20.00

(Get some tinsel from Christmas decorations, for display. Also look out for Indian cotton to use for drapes. Make a paper-flower garland.)

Buddhism Box

Buddha statue	£15.00
Rosewood prayer beads	£5.00
Buddhist postcards/ cards	£ 5.00
TOTAL:	£20.00

(Use plain brown or orange drapes for your display.)

Sikhism Box

Turban length	£ 6.00
Kangha (comb)	£ 1.00
Kara (bangle)	£ 1.50
Khanda (Sikh symbol)	£ 1.50
Miniature kirpan	£ 1.00
Picture of Guru Nanak	£ 2.00
Picture of Guru Gobind Singh	£ 2.00
TOTAL:	£15.00

(Find some bright orange material for drapes.)

Index of Artefacts and Images